THE NEW COMPLETE
GERMAN SHEPHERD DOG

Ch. Cobert's Reno of Lakeside, ROM
Owned by Vito Moreno and Connie Beckhardt

The NEW Complete

GERMAN SHEPHERD DOG

by JANE G. BENNETT

Past Editor, German Shepherd Dog Review
Official publication of the German Shepherd Dog Club of America

FIFTH EDITION
—Completely Revised—
Second Printing—1983

HOWELL BOOK HOUSE, Inc.
230 Park Avenue, New York, N.Y. 10169

Library of Congress Cataloging in Publication Data

Bennett, Jane G.
  The new Complete German shepherd dog.

  Rev. ed. of: The complete German shepherd dog /
Milo Denlinger. New ed. rev. 1970.

  Bibliography: p. 256.
  1. German shepherd dogs. I. Denlinger, Milo Grange,
1890-1953. The complete German shepherd dog. II. Title.
SF429.G37B46   1982   636.7'3   82-1031
ISBN 0-87605-151-4   AACR2

*This book is dedicated to
my husband and best friend,*

Tom,

whose lifelong hobby became mine also fifty years ago. His constant support during the thirty years I served as editor of the German Shepherd Dog Review *made that position much easier for me.*

With unswerving devotion, he has placed the best interests of the breed ahead of personal benefits. He has been uncompromising in his breeding, exhibiting and judging—and this integrity has been an inspiration to many.

Young Morgan Crooks, son of Philip and Salle Crooks of Stalwart Hills Farm, in a rapt moment with his friends.

Contents

Foreword — *by Robert E. Hamilton,* past president of the
    German Shepherd Dog Club of America   11

Chapter 1.   Origin and Early History in Germany   15

2.   Early Development in America   23

3.   The Breed in America Today   49
    Register of Merit Sires and Dams, 53;
    Active ROM Sires, 55; Inactive ROM Sires, 59;
    Active ROM Dams, 83; Inactive ROM Dams, 85

4.   The Grand Victors and Grand Victrixes — U.S.A.   95
    Grand Victors, 97; Grand Victrixes, 115
    Obedience Victors and Victrixes, 129

5.   Official Breed Standard of the
    German Shepherd Dog   133

6.   Blueprint of the German Shepherd Dog   141
    Why A Standard of Perfection?, 142
    Judging Your Dog, 147; Type, 148; Size, 151
    The Head, 152; Teeth, 153; Ears, 154; Eyes, 154
    Proportion, 155; The Neck, 155; The Body, 156
    Structural Faults (illustrated), 157
    The Front, 163; The Rear, 169
    Coat, 173; Dewclaws, 175
    A Picture of Your Dog, 176
    Gait, 177; Style, 182; Evaluation of Faults, 182

7.   Character of the German Shepherd Dog   187
    Temperament, 189
    Obedience Training, 191
    Schutzhund (Protection Dog) Training, 197

8.   The Most Utilitarian Dog of All   201
        Protection, 201; Police Dog, 203;
        Bomb Detector Dog, 204; Drug Detector Dog, 207;
        Guide Dog, 208; Search and Rescue, 211;
        Military Dogs, 217;
        New Services for New Times, 221

9.   The Breed in Germany Today   223
        Contrast of American and German Controls, 224
        Glossary of German Terms, 225

10.   The Siegers and Siegerins — Germany   231

11.   Health and Care   241
        Feeding Your Puppy, 244;
        Tips on Care, 245; Health, 247;
        Glossary of Dog Terms, 251

AUTHOR'S NOTE:

Sections of the text of Chapters 1, 2, 6, 9 and 11, are from earlier editions of this book (*The Complete German Shepherd Dog*), and were written by Milo G. Denlinger, Anne F. Paramoure and Gerda M. Umlauff. All text has been edited and updated for this edition.

—J.G.B.

Ch. Lakeside's Gilligan's Island winning Best in Show at Bryn Mawr Kennel Club under judge Alva Rosenberg. At the time of his premature death in 1972, "Gilly" was the top winning dog of all breeds in America. He won 5 Bests in Show in the six weeks immediately preceding his death. Bred by Daniel Dwier of Marlton, N.J., he won his first major at 6 months and was Futurity Victor at a year and a half. He was sold in 1971 to Helene Klotzman, who campaigned him extensively, with Kim Knoblauch handling. Gilligan appealed to all breed and specialty judges alike, compiling a record that included 36 all breed Bests in Show, 87 Working Group Firsts, 18 Specialty Bests of Breed and a total of 151 BOBs. —*Gilbert*

Club president Robert E. Hamilton, at left, at the 1976 German Shepherd Dog Club of America specialty, at which judge Ralph S. Roberts selected Ch. Padechma's Persuasion, owned by Margaretha P. Cunningham, as Grand Victor.

Foreword

by Robert E. Hamilton

Mr. Hamilton served as president of the German Shepherd Dog Club of America for five years, and has been a member of its Board of Directors intermittently since 1969. A long time judge of the breed, he has been a breeder and exhibitor since 1953. He is a charter member of the Grand Canyon German Shepherd Dog Club and of the Scottsdale Dog Fanciers Association, and has served both clubs as President.

THE GERMAN SHEPHERD DOG, because of its unique versatility, remains near the top of the popularity list. One of the resultant problems with this popularity is an almost totally uneducated approach to a proper breeding program on the part of many so-called breeders.

The development of a sound breeding program takes years of careful, selective and sometimes brutal planning. The acceptable German Shepherd Dog is a rare combination of conformation and character. The utilitarian virtues of the dog are the main criteria of its beauty.

I hope that this book, through its emphasis on these virtues, will help keep breeders aimed in the right direction.

I know of no individual more qualified than Jane Bennett to author this timely and informative book. Her background reads like a Who's Who of Shepherdom. She has been actively involved with the breed since 1937.

In 1948 the Board of Directors of the German Shepherd Dog Club of America selected Jane as the editor of its monthly publication. Dur-

A younger Bob Hamilton with Ch. Yuccasand's Bernina, owned by him and his wife Betty. Bernina was a daughter of 1952 Grand Victor Ingo Wunschelrute.

ing the 31 years that preceded her retirement in 1979, she elevated the *German Shepherd Dog Review* from a modest 500 subscribers to over 6,000 worldwide and won many awards along the way.

With but a single exception, she has attended every National Specialty since 1938 and has attended hundreds of shows in every area of this country as well as in Europe. She now serves as a member of the Board of Directors of the German Shepherd Dog Club of America, and is the club's official Delegate to the American Kennel Club.

I think you will agree with me that Jane brings a singularly unique background to her latest journalistic endeavor. Those of us dedicated to the advancement and improvement of this great breed are grateful to her for sharing her years of tireless dedication with us.

A timber wolf (*Canis lupus*). Until 1930, the German Shepherd Dog was known as the Alsatian Wolfdog in England. This, coupled with the breed's similarity in coloring and appearance, has led to a belief by some that the Shepherd is descended from the wolf. Actually whatever common ancestry they share would go back to the prehistoric Tomarctus of some 15 million years ago. It is more likely that the breed became known as the wolfdog because as a shepherd in earlier times he protected man and his sheep from the ravaging of wolves. — Photo, courtesy of *The Illustrated Encyclopedia of the Animal Kingdom,* The Danbury Press.

Captain Max von Stephanitz
"Father of the German Shepherd Dog"

1

Origin and Early History in Germany

THE GERMAN SHEPHERD DOG is a comparative newcomer to the world of the purebred. To understand this it is necessary to know briefly something about the history of the breed in Germany, the country of its birth.

The shepherds of Germany had used dogs with their flocks time out of mind, but they were dogs of no specific breed and type. In various parts of the country there was some tendency toward empiric uniformity, but it was not marked. In the flat plains of the north a small, fast dog sufficed; in the mountains south, a larger, more substantial dog (probably derived from the same stock as the Rottweiler) was needed. Long dogs, tall dogs, short dogs, low dogs, prick-eared dogs, any kind of dog that would do the work—all were lumped as shepherd dogs.

Even such soundness as these nondescripts possessed was a fortuitous thing. Unsound dogs, as a lot, were unable to do as much work as a herdsman as were sound dogs. Some unsound dogs—cow-hocked, or loose shouldered, or soft backed, or bandy legged—worked admirably despite their deformities, and were bred from. Looks counted for nothing at all; the sole criterion was the dog's ability to perform its tasks.

It was late in the nineteenth century that anything whatever was done about developing uniformity and beauty in this heterogeneous congeries of shepherds' dogs. The world was already beginning to grow smaller; communications were faster and easier; no longer did a pocket in the mountains protect men or dogs from outside influences. This movement to combine the dogs of the various parts of the country into a definite breed with a definite type was sporadic and half-hearted, but it was deliberately undertaken to improve the methods of herding sheep.

It led to the formation of the *Verein fur Deutsche Schafer-hunde S.V.,* which was established in April of 1899 during the Karlsruhe Exhibition. The moving spirits in the organization were Herr Artur Meyer and Rittmeister (cavalry captain) Max von Stephanitz, who was the first president. Von Stephanitz was an opinionated disciplinarian. However, we certainly admire the old man's enthusiasm and talents for organization. In a few short years the Verein, absolutely dominated by von Stephanitz, through careful selection and in-breeding, had molded the amorphous mass of herding dogs in Germany into the uniform, beautiful, sapient and useful breed we know as the German Shepherd Dog.

Von Stephanitz was adamant in his demands of utility and intelligence in the breed. In its utility and intelligence, according to him, lay a dog's beauty, and it had no beauty aside from those qualities. The standard was and is designed to describe the kind of dog fittest for herd service; and von Stephanitz saw to it that no German should ever entertain any other ideal for the breed. Any added beauty for beauty's sake was considered by von Stephanitz and his followers as beside the point. Of any attribute a dog might possess, von Stephanitz's only question was whether it might aid or hinder the dog in his work.

While it retarded the acceptance of the breed in other countries for many years, it was not a disservice to the German Shepherd Dog. This intense concern with fundamentals enabled the breeders to construct their canine work machine just so much more rapidly. Aesthetics, von Stephanitz did not concern himself about. Efficiency, efficiency, always efficiency. Having developed an efficient machine, von Stephanitz later tolerated, however grudgingly, some effort to develop show beauty in the dogs, but he insisted until the end that efficiency should take precedence over mere beauty.

With the tremendous spread of the breed and the lack of opportunities to work dogs with the flocks, the true old-time work of our dogs — service as a shepherd — became impossible for the majority of owners. In view of which, von Stephanitz decided to encourage the breed in other fields of work.

As transition he introduced, during the early years, training contests in which the dogs were tested for obedience and activity.

An early type of shepherd dog from central Germany.

From these, important divisions of work developed very early. Herr von Stephanitz pleaded for the use of dogs by the police and other authorities. At first his efforts were opposed and laughed at. But he kept at it unflaggingly, and eventually succeeded in getting various authorities to introduce the use of dogs for police service. When we view the wide use of dogs in service duty today, not only in Germany but throughout the world, we must newly admire the achievement of von Stephanitz. Younger fanciers now take it for granted, but older fanciers remember well the difficult negotiations and struggles that had to be carried on in behalf of the service dog. Because of his pioneer work in this field, the Captain—along with other honors—must be regarded as Father of the dog service system.

It was clearly proper that the largest specialty club should also be called to play an authoritative role in the general affairs of dog-dom. But, as so frequently happens in life to those whose labor has achieved great success, it was attacked and vilified. Envy and malice played their part here also in rendering the task of Herr von Stephanitz more difficult. But in his case his opponents had caught the wrong man; and while in defense he often struck hard, it was not out of personal vindictiveness but only to further the success of the view in which he believed. Here also he won the victory. In the

17

Horand von Grafrath (SZ-1), the first registered German Shepherd Dog in the SV stud book. Horand, originally named Hektor v. Linksrhein, was renamed when acquired by Captain von Stephanitz.

Hektor v. Schwaben, SZ-13, HGH, German Grand Champion for 1900 and 1901. A son of Horand von Grafrath.

Deutschen Kartell für Hundewesen, of which the SV was among the charter members, Herr von Stephanitz had a decisive influence. His executive ability also bore fruit here. And in the *Reichsrerband für das Deutsche Hundewesen* he was a valued collaborator whose word carried weight.

There were essentially three strains utilized in the founding of the breed: the Thuringia Strain, the Wurttemburg Strain and the Krone Strain. It is vain at this time to go into the various early dogs and how they were produced. The strains have since become so muddled and mixed up through crossing and recrossing that it is impossible to detect the attributes of any particular one or particular strain of these earlier dogs in the dogs we have today. It serves no purpose here to trace the ancestry of the breed to its earliest exponents, although it is interesting to consider how profound an influence, through inbreedings, a few individuals have had upon the breed. Emerging from these early dogs we find a group of dominant dogs, which includes the first registered dog of the breed—Horand von Grafrath (originally named Hektor von Linksrhein, but renamed after he was acquired by Captain von Stephanitz), Hektor von Schwaben (a son of Horand and the German Sieger for 1900 and 1901), Dewett Barbarosso, Beowulf, Roland von Starkenburg and Graf Eberhard von Hohen Esp.

These dogs are found in the pedigrees of the earlier American dogs. Many in particular trace to Roland von Starkenburg (the 1906 and 1907 Sieger), especially through his son, Hettel Uckermark (the 1909 Sieger). Roland was a grandson of Hektor von Schwaben on his sire's side, and a great-grandson on his dam's side. When it is considered how intensely inbred these early dogs were, it is easy to understand their profound influence upon their breed.

There is a temptation, which must be resisted, to go on and tell something about the famous early German dogs that never came to America and the distinct strains formed by them; especially about the Kriminalpolizei, the Boll, and the exquisite Riedekenburgs, about Horst von Boll, the most bred-to dog of his time; about Tell and Yung Tell von Kriminalpolizei; and most of all about Flora Berkemeyer, founding matron of the Riedekenburg Strain, to which we are indebted for the class and beauty of our present-day dogs. Flora was something of a mutation toward the beautiful. Her progeny played a principal part in establishing the delicacy, grace, beauty and sensitiveness that has made the breed acceptable as show dogs and so popular throughout the world.

Roland v. Starkenburg, SZ-1537, German Grand Champion for 1906 and 1907. Virtually all German Shepherd Dog pedigrees in America trace back to Roland. He was a grandson of Hektor v. Schwaben on his sire's side, and a great-grandson on his dam's side.

Hettel Uckermark, SZ-3897, German Grand Champion for 1909. A son of Roland v. Starkenburg and very important in early American pedigrees.

The *Verein für Deutsche Schaferhunde* became big business, with more than fifty thousand members and over six hundred branches. It was the largest and best organized association of breeders pertaining to a single breed in the entire world. It kept and published a stud book of the breed and published its semi-monthly Gazette, which was sent to all its members. It held its "Sieger Show," at which the top German Shepherd Dogs—one male and one bitch—were named.

The *Verein* assumed jurisdiction over breeding and breeding practices, undertook to declare what dogs were fit to breed from and what dogs were unfit, and went so far as to dictate what dogs should be bred to what bitches and to forbid the rearing of more than a stated number of puppies from each litter. It forbade the breeding of bitches before a stated age, and set a maximum age at which a dog could be employed at stud. It was parental in its attitude toward breeders, authoritarian, doctrinal and dictatorial. *Verein* laws were immutable and inflexible. It was typically German, with its hierarchy of authority, which was not to be gainsaid or questioned.

The breeders became mere automatons to carry out the mandates of the *Verein*, which they accepted uncritically. In the breed's beginning this concerted action was valuable; it was largely responsible for the rapidity with which a vast number of amorphous dogs were transformed into a uniform breed.

American breeders took seriously the dicta of the *Verein*, and sought to accept its authority. German "authorities" were invited to America to judge and to make "surveys" of the dogs. American breeders hung on to the words of these judges as if they had been chiseled on stone and handed down from Sinai.

Von Stephanitz wrote an ostensibly learned book, which was translated into English and published in 1923 under the title *The German Shepherd Dog in Word and Picture,* and was widely circulated. It was an impressive tome of more than 700 pages and purported to tell all. It was in fact an assemblage of valid information and misinformation, outmoded scientific theories, and personal and racial prejudices. It was verbose and turgid. It is only natural that von Stephanitz should have written about the breed in Germany and under German conditions, but many Americans sought to apply it to American conditions.

Despite the aging author's good nature and heavy humor, the book was distasteful to many American readers and in the long run did the breed much harm. To Americans *their dogs are a means to*

Flora Berkemeyer, founding matron of the Riedekenburg strain. Her progeny contributed very importantly to the grace and beauty that the German Shepherd Dog exhibits in the rings today.

an end, not an end in themselves. Americans are individualists and do not succumb to authoritarianism. They have no wish to be dictated to; they want to do things in their own way.

2

Early Development in America

THE FIRST RECORDED REFERENCE to a German Shepherd Dog in America was when Mira of Dalmore (never registered), property of the Dalmore Kennels of H.A. Dalrymple, of Port Allegheny, Pennsylvania, was exhibited. She was first, Open class, at Newcastle, and first, Open, Philadelphia. These awards were probably in the Miscellaneous Classes at those shows, for we find the same bitch appearing and winning the Miscellaneous Class at New York in 1907, entered as a Belgium (sic) Sheepdog.

The bitch's real name was Mira von Offingen, imported by Otto H. Gross in 1906, along with two others. How she came to be shown in Dalrymple's name is not known. However, Gross brought her over, and, as nobody in America appeared to be interested in the breed, he eventually took her back to Germany. Her picture indicates a somewhat doggy bitch with very large ears, great bone, and generally of good type.

Mira of Dalmore was never registered in the American Kennel Club Studbook, and probably went neglected and unappreciated. She was bred from the very best blood of the era, being by Beowulf out of Hella von Schwaben, sister to Hektor von Schwaben. She was whelped July 12, 1905, and was bred by one P. Stetter.

She was again exhibited in the Miscellaneous Class at New York in 1908, this time entered as a German Sheepdog. In this class she had competition within her own breed, another German Sheepdog, known sim-

Nina Dexter, pioneer German Shepherd Dog breeder in the West, with Ch. Gilda v. Doernhoft and Ernani v. Graustein.

ply as Queen, being exhibited by Adolph Vogt, who won first in her class, defeating Mira. This Queen was, in all probability, Queen of Switzerland 115006, of largely Krone blood, the first German Sheepdog to be registered in the Studbook of the American Kennel Club.

The classification of Mira of Dalmore as a Belgian Sheepdog in the New York show in 1907 is not strange. There appears to have been little distinction between the Belgian and the German Shepherd Dogs at that time in America. As late as 1912 the two breeds were lumped together in some show classifications, although they were kept separate in the studbook. This made little difference since they were exhibited in Miscellaneous Classes.

The year 1912 is noteworthy in the annals of the German Shepherd Dog, since it the year in which Benjamin H. Throop, of Scranton, Pennsylvania, and Miss Anne Tracy, of Highland Falls-on-Hudson, New York, each registered their first dogs of the breed. These two ardent fanciers are all but forgotten and unknown to the current generation of fanciers of the German Shepherd Dog, but they were the moving spirits in the organization of the German Shepherd Dog Club of America in 1913. There were 26 charter members, of which Mrs. C. Halstead Yates was named president; F. Empkin, vice-president; and Benjamin H. Throop, secretary.

The breed was Miss Tracy's premier interest and she was indefatigable in her propagation of the faith in it. She owned one of the first two champions of record in America, Luchs (or Lux), 161964; the other being Herta von Ehrangrund, 163047, property of the Winterview Kennels of L.I. De Winter of Suttenburg, New Jersey, for many years a prominent exhibitor at Eastern shows and ardent supporter of the club and of the breed. These championships were made in the same year (1913) and it is impossible to know which takes precedence over the other.

Championships made prior to 1917 mean little in any event, since a show's rating was determined by the entire number of dogs of all breeds exhibited, and a single exhibit received the same number of points as the most numerous breed in the show. Many champions in obscure breeds were made without any competition whatever. Moreover, the judging was, to put the matter mildly, "spotty" until well into the twenties. Few judges knew the standard and what it meant, and they were sadly reluctant to learn. Many of the judges were British or at least Anglophile and scornful of anything of German origin. They gave their prizes to dogs as square as possible and as big as possible. One well-known judge, in a printed critique as late as 1917, went on record as having set a dog back in his class because of his length. Show awards, looked at in a most objective way, were preposterous.

The German Shepherd Dog Club of America staged its first specialty show, at Greenwich, Connecticut, June 11, 1915, with 40 dogs benched and four points toward championship. Miss Tracy was the judge. She again judged the show of the same club in New York City on November 16 of the following year, when 96 dogs were benched. The point rating had been revised and the show carried only four points again, despite the more than doubled entry.

The foremost stud dog of the period was Nero Affolter, property of Mr. Throop's Elmview Kennels. Nero was a tremendous, square, common kind of dog, who won at some shows and was far down in the prize list at others. It was doubtless his size that made him such a favorite. He had little else to recommend him, and his blood, despite his quondam popularity, has been weeded well out of America's strains.

The first truly great dog to come to America was Champion Apollo von Hunenstein, 182499, imported by Elmview in 1914. He was whelped February 20, 1912, and had become the Austrian and Belgian champion of the year 1913, French and German champion of the year 1914. He easily won his American championship, but was neglected in the stud in favor of Nero Affolter, his kennelmate. He had been mated in Germany before shipment to the greatest of all brood bitches up to that time, Flora Berkemeyer, and was sire of her most successful litter, which included Dorte, Diethelm, Danko, Drusus, and Dulo von Riedekenburg; and so his merits as a stud dog were not unknown.

Apollo was different from the dogs that had previously come to America, distinctly of the correct and modern type, a long dog of tremendous quality and refinement. He was before his time and American fanciers did not appreciate him until it was too late to avail themselves of his services. We can only speculate what a blood foundation he might have laid, if only he had been utilized.

Upon the untimely death of Mr. Throop, about 1923, Apollo passed into the safekeeping of the Joselle Kennels of Peter A. B. Widener of Elkins Park, Pennsylvania, where he was given the best of care until his death. His mounted body went to the Peabody Museum of Yale University, where it may now be seen. Mr. Widener did not undervalue Apollo so much as he overvalued Dolf von Dustern-brook, the German Sieger of 1920, a grandson of Apollo through Dorte von Riedekenburg. We shall hear more of Widener and Dolf anon.

The Oak Ridge Kennels of Thomas Fortune Ryan came into the picture in 1913, with Oak Ridge Alarich von der Alpenluft, and a host of other dogs. Alarich was a significant dog for his day, but only for his day, which was short. The Ryan interest in the breed was even shorter, and his best dogs soon passed to Mr. and Mrs. Halsted Yates. Yates was at the time superintendent of the Ryan Oak Ridge estate. Subsequently Alarich became the property of Mrs. Alvin Untermeyer, who was later to be an important factor in Shepherd Dogs on the West Coast.

It was at about that period that John Gans' Hoheluft Kennels entered the lists, with dogs that were not good enough. He was later to be heard from with some of the greatest German Shepherd Dogs ever and was active until 1951.

Early in 1917 America entered the World War, and all things of German origin suddenly became taboo. Even before the entry of this country into the War, sympathy for the British cause had injured the

26

Ch. Hamilton Anni v. Humboldtpark, German Siegerin for 1919 and 1920. Imported by Hamilton Farms.

German Siegerin for 1922, 1923 and 1924, American Grand Victrix for 1926, Ch. Asta v. d. Kaltenweide, SchH.

interests of German breed dogs; but after America's entrance into the war, the German Shepherd Dog shared the obloquy of the Dachshund, Beethoven's symphonies, Wagner's operas, Goethe's poetry, Frankfurter sausages, sauerkraut, and hamburger steak.

The official name of the breed, allotted to it by the American Kennel Club, had been the German Sheepdog, although the member club that sponsored the breed was known as the German Shepherd Dog Club of America. In an effort to save the breed from the vengeance of the super-patriots, the American Kennel Club changed its official name to Shepherd Dog, without any reference to its German origin, just as it changed the name of the Dachshund to Badger Dog. The change did little to allay the furor. Nobody was fooled. The sponsoring club was even prevailed upon to drop "German" from its name.

The prejudice against things German abated with the signing of the armistice in 1918. Nobody any longer held the country of its origin against the German Shepherd Dog. American soldiers returned from Europe with incredible tales of the intelligence, beauty, usefulness and wisdom of the dogs that they had seen. Strongheart and Rin-Tin-Tin were starred in the silent pictures. Everybody wanted, and almost everybody had, a German Shepherd Dog. However, it was not until 1931 that the word "German" was restored to the name of the club that sponsored the breed and to the breed itself. The word "shepherd" was retained in the name; it did not revert to German Sheepdog, but became the German Shepherd Dog, as it should have been from the beginning. The breed is one of the relatively few that have the word *dog* as part of their official AKC designation.

Fortunately, in the Second World War the animosity of Americans was reasonably confined to the German Government, to Hitler, and Nazism. Beethoven's music was not forbidden, and German breeds of dogs did not have to suffer for German behavior. Dachsunds flourished. Boxers grew popular, and German Shepherd Dogs were frankly German. The American mind had grown more mature and did not surrender itself to the racial hysteria that had animated it in the former struggle.

With all the vain effort in America to deny the breed its German birthright, the nomenclature situation in Britian was even worse. There was an equal upsurge of interest in the breed in Britain, where it was first known as the Alsatian Wolfdog. The breed was not Alsatian in it origin, and there is nothing wolf-like about it.

The "wolfdog" part of the name was recognized to interfere with its popularity, and was soon discarded. However, the breed was, until 1979, known in Britain as the Alsatian, a misnomer as great as that of the Great Dane, which is not a Danish dog but a German. In that year the English Kennel Club finally submitted to appeals of British breeders and the World Union of German Shepherd Dog Clubs and recognized the breed's proper name and origin.

But let's get back to the breed's development following World War I. The German Shepherd Dog pot was on the fire and was getting pretty hot. Everybody wanted a Shepherd (or Police Dog as it was erroneously called), but only the very rich for the most part could afford one. In the fall of 1920, Peter A. B. Widener II imported Dolf von Dusternbrook, 289407, to whose name Widener prefixed his kennel name of Joselle. Dolf, whelped April 16, 1918, was by Luchs von Uckermark out of Dorte von Riedekenburg, a member of Flora Berkemeyer's litter by Apollo von Hunenstein. Dolf had been Sieger (Grand Champion) of Germany for the year 1919, and Grand Champion of Austria 1920. He was a sensation in America, defeating every German Shepherd Dog he ever met, and was many times best dog of all breeds in the show. Widener is alleged to have paid $10,000 for Dolf and a bitch shown as Joselle's Debora von Weimar, an unheard of price at the time.

The Joselle Kennels at Elkins Park, Pennsylvania, besides Dolf and Apollo von Hunenstein, housed some notable bitches, the greatest of the breed. Dolf was not the success at stud that his record in the show ring might have warranted.

But he was in competition in the stud with Hamilton Erich von Grafenwerth, 323540, imported early in 1921 and owned by the Hamilton Farms Kennels of J.C. Brady, at Gladstone, New Jersey. Erich was some three months younger than Dolf, having been whelped July 7, 1918. He was by Alex von Westfalenheim out of Bianca von Riedekenburg, who was by Hettel Uckermark out of Flora Berkemeyer. Erich had been Sieger of Germany for 1920, and was the dog of his time. He had a tremendous show career in America. But more than a mere show dog, here was a stud. The largest part of the fine dogs to come from Germany for years claimed Erich as sire or grandsire. He was utilized in America as his merits deserved, and sired most of the best dogs that were bred on this side of the ocean. Erich had everything, and transmitted it to his get. He was utterly invaluable.

Along with Erich at Hamilton Farms was the noteworthy bitch

29

Hamilton Anni vom Humboldtpark, Siegerin of Germany for two successive years, 1919 and 1920, besides being the Holland female champion for 1919. Hamilton Farms housed many lesser lights, but these two were tops.

Erich and Anni had been brought to America for Hamilton Farms by Otto Gross. Subsequently, Erich was sold to Mrs. M. Hartley Dodge's Giralda Farms, and spent his last years there at Madison, New Jersey.

Then early in 1922 the Hoheluft Kennels of John Gans, of Staten Island, New York, in cooperation with the Rexden-Belcarza Kennels, a partnership of which Reginald M. Cleveland was the leading spirit, brought to America Geri von Oberklamm, 326000. Geri had been Grand Champion of Austria, but had missed out on the German Siegership because he was not gun-sure. He was somewhat older than the others, having been whelped August 31, 1917. He was by Arnim von Riedekenburg, a member of the Flora Berkemeyer's litter by Kuno Edelweiss, her first. Geri's dam was Alice vom Karlspring, by Billo von Riedekenburg, from Flora's Hettel Uckermark litter. Thus Geri was a grandson of Flora on the one side and a great-grandson on the other.

He was a superb dog, of great size, impressive, refined, sensitive, and beautiful. Above all was his ability to move. How that dog could move! It was a joy to watch him cover ground. Like clockwork.

Geri had been extensively bred from in Germany before his exportation, and he was widely, if not always judiciously, used in America. There was somewhere in his germ-plasm a shy streak, for a good many of his progeny were over-sensitive. He also tended to transmit a good many soft ears. Despite these failings, he was a stud dog par excellence. His progeny as a lot were notably sound and moved magnificently. Geri chafed at kennel life, and subsequently was sold to Mrs. Elliott Dexter, in whose California home he ruled as the kingpin, regained his spirits, and did the Western fancy a vast good.

The fourth of the quartet of great dogs was Cito Bergerslust, 350000, born December 28, 1920, who was Sieger of Germany for 1922, and was purchased by John Gans late the same year. Cito was a son of Geri and resembled his sire in many respects, especially in his ability to cover ground. His dam was Goda von Munsdorf, by Alex Westfalenheim out of a daughter of Billo von Riedekenburg, giving him three crosses of Flora Berkemeyer. Cito was the top dog in America

Int. Grand Champion Geri von Oberklamm, PH, imported to America by John Gans, Hoheluft Kennels.

Ch. Cito Bergerslust, SchH, German Sieger 1922 and 1923, U.S. Grand Victor 1924 and 1925. Imported to America by John Gans.

for several years, was bred to extensively, but not so much as his merits warranted.

Dolf, Erich, and Geri had all been whelped during the War. It is to be remembered that Germany was not devastated, not even invaded, in the First World War, as it was in the Second, but it will ever remain a mystery how the Germans succeeded in turning out these supreme dogs, in addition to others only slightly inferior to them, and many magnificent bitches, in the hurly-burly of a war that was depleting the country's entire economy.

There is no mystery as to why the Germans were willing to sell such paragons. In the early twenties inflation was at its height in Germany. One American dollar was worth millions of marks. A few thousand American dollars meant luxury and independence. The buyers were all men of great wealth.

A notable thing about these dogs is that the three older ones were all grand-progeny of Flora Berkemeyer, and the fourth was the product of three crosses of Flora's blood. Most of the great bitches that came over in the same era and the only slightly inferior dogs were bred along the same lines—Flora Berkemeyer, usually combined with Uckermark blood, particularly with Alex Westfalenheim. Flora is an instance of a bitch (which, as compared with a dog, is capable of producing only a limited number of progeny) influencing a whole breed for its betterment. It is she and she alone that explains the vast output of fine German dogs in the era.

In the summer of 1921, Bruno Hoffman of the Protection Kennels, White Plains, New York, imported Etzel von Oeringen, 285737, a dog that was to become famous as a motion picture star under the name of Strongheart. During his motion picture career Etzel was the property of Jane Murfin, an actor and writer, and Larry Trimble, who trained the dog for pictures. Etzel had been whelped in Germany, October 1, 1917, and had been completely trained for police service. It was Trimble's job to untrain the dog of his police regimentation, and retrain him for the pictures. The success of the new star was instantaneous and sensational. Everybody wanted a dog just like him, and believed that just any German Shepherd Dog would exhibit feats of sagacity like those of Strongheart in the pictures. He was a good dog without being a great dog, a handsome, upstanding animal, but lacking in the essentials of German Shepherd Dog type. The acting was of course three-fourths Trimble and one-fourth dog. However, the advent of Strongheart gave a greater impetus to the

Int. Champion Dolf von Duesternbrook, PH, German Sieger for 1919 and U.S. Grand Victor, 1923. Owned by Peter A.B. Widener's Joselle Kennels.

Int. Ch. Hamilton v. Grafenwerth, PH, German Sieger 1920 and U.S. Grand Champion 1922. An exceptional sire, he was imported by Hamilton Farms in 1921, and acquired by Giralda Farms in his later years.

Strongheart (Etzel von Oeringen).

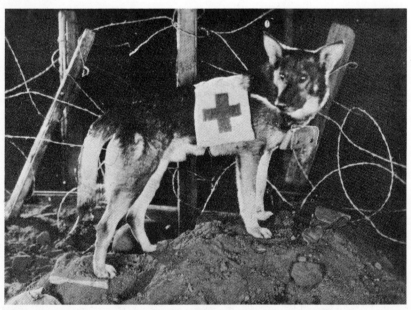

Rin Tin Tin, pictured here as a casualty dog locating the wounded in "Find Your Man", became the most famous of all canine movie stars. Rinty was a most effective performer and often won critical acclaim for his "acting", such as this from a review of "The Night Cry": "He plays one whole scene in closeup, literally registering hope and sorrow by a drooping of his ears and a moistening of his eyes."

popularity of the breed than any other single event to that time.

Etzel von Oeringen (Strongheart) was a son of Nores von der Kriminalpolizei, 318118, a dog born March 15, 1915, and sire of some notable but overrated Shepherds, such as Grimm von der Mainkur, Deborah von Weimar, Dora von Rheinwald, and the 1921 German Grand Champion Harras von der Juch, as well as Strongheart. Nores was a Boll bred dog, without a trace of Flora Berkemeyer. He was not too well angulated in the shoulder, and the last section of his tail was missing, a hereditary fault seen in many offspring of Nores.

Nonetheless, he was touted as a great sire, and in the summer of 1921 Lawrence H. Armour, Lake Forest, Illinois, imported Nores to head his Green Bay Kennels. Everybody wanted a brother to Strongheart and Nores was much bred to for this reason, as well as for his reputation as the sire of winners. He was not a success in the stud in America, however, and is introduced here only because he was so much used and talked about. Most of his progeny were upright in shoulder, and a percentage of them were short of tail and were a dead loss. Fading pigment, an influence particularly seen in the Midwest, came through this line. The Nores influence is now happily weeded from the breed and we hear no more of him.

Lee Duncan, returning from service in World War I, brought back with him from France a puppy that was to become famous as Rin Tin Tin. This dog could not be registered as he had only one generation of pedigree. He was bred by a Captain Bryant, and was whelped January 15, 1919, by Fritz out of Betty. It is said that his dam was captured in the trenches.

While he was in training, he was exhibited a few times but took third in classes of three, and was not a show dog at all. However, under the able and loving tutelage of Duncan, Rinty achieved a fame far surpassing that of any show dog.

He became, of course, the most celebrated of all movie dogs. His tremendous popularity reinforced and then multiplied the impact that Strongheart had registered with the public.

In all, Rin Tin Tin made 19 films and their success is credited with keeping Warner Brothers studios afloat in the hard times before the advent of "talkies." For the most part, the films were well done, skillfully mixing action, comedy and sentiment. The basic idea was to involve Rinty in as many human dilemmas as possible.

Lee Duncan with a Rin Tin Tin of the mid-'50s.— *Van Pelt*

In one, for instance, he had to quickly choose whether to rescue the heroine or his canine lady friend. Some of the stories were rather naive. In *Clash of the Wolves*, he played a dog suspected of being a wolf. To disguise him, the hero fitted him out with a false beard. Walking through the town, the bearded dog was taken for granted. But then the beard fell off, he was immediately recognized, and the lynch mob was after him. And all of this was played straight.

Rin Tin Tin died in 1932, passing away (according to legend) in the lap of his admirer, Jean Harlow. A succession of Rintys followed, all trained by Lee Duncan. The last one (or ones, as several were used) appeared in a television serial of the 1950s, "The Adventures of Rin Tin Tin."

Another very popular movie dog, Bullet, with his owner, Roy Rogers. Holding Bullet's paw is Madeleine Baiter, a prominent German Shepherd Dog judge of the '50s.—*Osborne*

Proud family from the famous Cosalta Kennels of the late Miss Marie J. Leary. Starlight of Cosalta, ROM dam (at left) and Ch. Cosalta's Ace of Wynnewood, CDX, ROM sire (right), with their son who became Ch. Dark Night of Cosalta.

Marie J. Leary with Ch. Armin v. Salon, SchH III and holder of an American tracking title. Miss Leary's Cosalta Kennels, established in 1923, was one of the major German Shepherd Dog kennels through many years and a pioneer in Obedience.

In 1923 Miss Marie Leary established her Cosalta Kennels at Greenwich, Connecticut, and exhibited a dog known as Hector, which she had imported from France. The dog as an individual had no significance of his own, but he was the first Cosalta. Little was it dreamed at the time that Miss Leary was establishing what was to become one of the major kennels for the breed in the world. She turned out champion after champion, largely home bred, and continued to breed excellent dogs in great numbers until 1961.

Miss Leary's success was the more remarkable in that her dogs were largely American-bred and that they won despite an obvious judicial preference for imported dogs. There were American-bred dogs in abundance, but for their very top awards the judges turned largely to dogs of German origin. The glamor of importation seems to have played a considerable part in this, and it is not to be gainsaid that in the twenties the general run of American-breds were not as good as the foremost of the German dogs. Buying the greatest dogs that Germany could produce, the Americans appear not to have

39

An up-the-ladder assemblage of puppies from Cosalta Kennels.

known how best to utilize them. To this rule Miss Leary was a notable exception. She took advantage of the great imported studs and bred her bitches to them, and consistently produced dogs of a high order.

The same year of 1923 marked the introduction of dogs from the Giralda Farms Kennels of Mrs. M. Hartley Dodge of Madison, New Jersey. Mrs. Dodge's beginnings were made with high class stock, to be sure. However, the Lady of Giralda was soon to be in the very forefront of exhibitors, with such magnificent bitches as the 1926 Siegerin of Germany, Arna aus der Ehrenzelle, the Siegerin of Austria, Pia von Haus Schutting, and Giralda's Teuthilde von Hagenschiess. The first of the truly noteworthy stud dogs at Giralda was Iso von Doernerhof, but he was to be followed by many of the greatest dogs in the world.

Mrs. Dodge was a daughter of William Rockefeller, who was one of the founders of the American Kennel Club. Her tremendous for-

Two of the more important producers at Mrs. M. Hartley Dodge's Giralda Kennels. At top, Ch. Giralda's Iso v. Doernerhof, SchH, whelped 1922, a prepotent black who contributed strongly to the breed. Below, Dewet v.d. Starrenburg, SchH, whelped 1932, a Best in Show winning son of German Sieger Odin v. Stolzenfels.

The distinguished lady of Giralda, Mrs. M. Hartley Dodge, pictured awarding a trophy to Grant E. Mann, breeder-owner-handler of the 1946 Grand Victrix, Ch. Leda v. Liebestraum, ROM.

tune enabled her to acquire the dogs of her choice, (which turned out to be very judicious) and to provide a large number of dogs with accommodations and care such as dogs seldom receive. Mrs. Dodge did not exhibit dogs as extensively as some other kennels. She cared less about show records than about the possession of a magnificent lot of dogs. Her ardent love of dogs and interest in their betterment prompted her in 1927 to establish the great Morris and Essex Dog Show, which was held annually (until 1957) on the polo field of her Giralda Farms estate. It was the largest outdoor dog show in the world, and set a record for the most entries at an American show (5,002 entries in behalf of 4,456 different dogs in 1939) that still stands at this writing.

Artist's depiction of Ch. Giralda's Lola, CD (whelped 1928) and family.

The Morris and Essex show, held on Mrs. Dodge's estate, at Madison, N.J., was America's largest outdoor show over many years. Ch. Odin v. Busecker-Schloss is seen winning one of the two Group firsts he registered at the show, this in 1941.

Ch. Klodo von Boxberg, 1925 German Sieger, Klodo, a son of Ch. Erich v. Grafenwerth, was an influential early sire. Owned by William Goldbecker.

In late 1926 the Maraldene Kennels of Hamden, Connecticut, imported the German Sieger Klodo von Boxberg, 551052, which subsequently went to a Mr. Kane in Chicago. Klodo a comparatively small dog, without any exaggeration of type, would hardly be noticed except by the German Shepard Dog expert. He was one of those plain and undistinguished dogs, but so superbly constructed that there was little fault to find with him. One of the notable things about him was that he was a son of Erich von Grafenwerth, and had been whelped August 20, 1921.

In 1929, the Mardex Kennels imported Utz von Haus Schutting, 707401, whelped March 12, 1926, another German Sieger and son of Klodo von Boxberg. He was out of a bitch by Falco von Indetal, another son of Erich from a daughter of Billo von Riedekenburg. Utz had another cross of Flora Berkemeyer on his dam's side through Diethelm von Riedekenburg. Utz was a small dog of exceptional excellence, and his Erich blood was to tell in a host of superb progeny. He was used on many Cosalta bitches.

The German Shepherd Dog had had its day of glory. All through the twenties the domestic production was unable to supply

44

the market for puppies, despite that the breed is very prolific. The Germans recognized a good thing when they saw it and dumped on the American market all kinds of nondescript dogs. People liked to talk about their importations. The fortunate few and discriminating obtained the best the Germans were able to turn out, but many others assumed that just any dog imported from Germany was a good one. Many were their disillusions.

The demand was satiated. Big dogs were a burden. The cost of their food was considerable. The depression set in and buyers were few. Puppies went begging. Entries in the breed in dog shows slackened off. All this was deemed to be harmful to the breed, but it turned out to be salutary. It purged the fancy of its triflers. True lovers of German Shepherd Dogs stuck with the breed, but they were on their own. There were few importations. If we were to have good dogs, Americans would have to breed them.

There are two particularly notable exceptions to that statement, however. In the summer of 1936 John Gans imported Sieger Pfeffer von Bern A-87262, whelped June 20, 1934. He was by Dachs

Utz v. Haus Schutting, Z Pr, German Sieger for 1929. A son of Ch. Klodo v. Boxberg, Utz was great-grandsire of Ch. Pfeffer v. Bern and Ch. Odin v. Busecker-Schloss. He was owned by Dexter Hewitt, Mardex Kennels.

The prepotent Ch. Pfeffer v. Bern, ROM, 1937 German Sieger and U.S. Grand Victor 1937 and 1938. Owned by John Gans, Hoheluft Kennels.

Ch. Odin v. Busecker-Schloss, ROM, also a major breeding influence of his time. Owned by Sidney F. Heckert, Jr.

von Bern, a grandson of Utz von Haus Schütting, and his dam was also by an Utz dog. We see how the Erich blood has carried on. Pfeffer just about revolutionized the breed in America. Champion after champion issued from his loins, many of them of such excellence as to stultify the best the Germans ever bred, with the exception of the great four, Dolf, Erich, Geri and Cito. Pfeffer von Bern sired literally hundreds of champions and winning dogs. The most famous and certainly one of the best of the Pfeffer get was Nox of Ruthland, A-350676, whelped May 16, 1939, bred and exhibited by the Ruthland Kennels, of Scarsdale, New York. Nox in his turn carried on the line with sons and grandsons and great-grandsons of the highest excellence.

The other noteworthy importation was Odin vom Busecker Schloss, A-262642, whelped April 23, 1934, and imported in the fall of 1938 by Mr. and Mrs. Sidney F. Heckert, Jr., of the Villa Marina Kennels at Santa Barbara, California. This was a tenstrike. The dog was extensively exhibited and rather consistently swept all before him. Again the Erich blood is in evidence, since Odin was a half brother to Pfeffer von Bern, being also by Dachs von Bern, a grandson of Utz, whereas the dam of Odin was a granddaughter of Klodo von Boxberg.

Odin was especially notable for his strength of back and transmission of power. He was a magnificent mover, especially at a rapid trot, Western breeders utilized him extensively with the most excellent results, and many of the wisest breeders of the Eastern seaboard sent their best bitches to his court.

Ernest Loeb has been one of the major figures on the German Shepherd Dog
scene in America for five decades. He is pictured handling Ch. Quell von Fredeholz, SchH III, ROM, a great dog he imported for Howard Newman, and who
was later owned by the all-rounder judge Anton Korbel. Quell was never defeated in the breed, winning 21 Bests of Breed, 21 Group Firsts, and 11 all-breed
Bests in Show. Mr. Loeb is now a highly respected judge.

3

The Breed
in America Today

I N THIS LIMITED SPACE it is impossible to touch upon, even to name, the hundreds of great breeders and thousands of great dogs we have had in America through the years, and continue to have today.

However, it will be recognized that certain kennels have made a particularly lasting impression upon the breed. The contributions of such kennels as Hoheluft, Giralda, Edgetowne, Benlore, San Miguel, Cosalta, Rocky Reach, Long-Worth, Liebestraum, Grafmar and Dornwald remain especially noteworthy. And closer to our own time, those of such kennels as: Arbywood, Beckgold, Caraland, Carolon, Cobert, Covina Knolls, Doppelt-Tay, Eko-Lan, Fran-Jo, Grossland, Hartwald, Hessian, Jet-Land, Lahngold, Llano-Estacado, Maur-ray, Peddacres, Pinebeach, Philberlyn, Sarego, Tucker-Hill, Von Nassau, Waldenmark and Wilva Don.

Present day kennels do not have as intense a dominance as did earlier strains. Today we find certain individual dogs credited with breed influence rather than bloodlines of particular kennels. Ease of transporting bitches to top stud dogs has broadened the breed base so that one dog's qualities are no longer confined to a small area.

Another factor has been the tremendous influx of German dogs in the years following World War II. After the first rush, American breeders became more selective in their use of these dogs. New blood

49

has erased the American-bred bloodlines in many areas, but intelligent use of dogs resulting from the best efforts of German breeders can be most advantageous. The names of Lord vom Zenntal, Quell vom Fredeholz, Bill vom Kleistweg, Troll vom Richterbach, Ulk Wikingerblut, Greif von Elfenhain, Bernd von Kallengarten, Kledo Eremitenklause, Condor vom Stoerstrudel, Harry vom Donakai, Axel von Poldihaus, Raps Piastendam, Cent von Funf Giebeln, Lido v. Johanneshauch, Treu vom Wolfstock, Bodo von Lierberg and Caralon's Hein von der Lockenheim identify imports whose influence will be felt for many years to come. A marked breed improvement has already been noted from the use of these dogs with the vast number of excellent American-bred bitches.

Today there are many, many small kennels producing far-above-average dogs and fewer enormous kennel operations. This trend is good for the breed since German Shepherd Dogs flourish best in a family situation. It is not a breed that lends itself readily to mass production. Most breeders confine themselves to working with a half dozen bitches and a dog or two. They find that in concentrating attention and care upon a few dogs, they obtain better results than by operating on a wholesale scale.

As we move into the Eighties, there is a greater effort to breed more uniformly to type. Exchange of ideas, travel to distant shows and meeting with other breeders, the various projects of the German Shepherd Dog Club of America, Inc. (such as the National Futurity Sweepstakes), the growth of regional clubs with their educational programs—all have helped to increase knowledge and to build toward breed goals.

There is still much to be done in this country to bring the breed to its zenith. Uniformity of type remains a goal to strive for. Temperament in many lines is far from admirable. Properly-angled shoulders are the exception. Teeth faults have happily diminished. Side gaits are better than average, but action coming and going needs improvement.

Much study, and proper attention to breeding partners, can correct a great deal in several generations. So, newcomers, beware of hit-or-miss breeding; having a litter of puppies is hard work, so make the project worthwhile. If your bitch is a healthy, typy German Shepherd Dog, breed her to the best male available. If she is not, have her spayed rather than clutter the dog population with more mediocre to less-than-average specimens.

Top honors at the 1952 German Shepherd Dog Club of America Specialty were swept by dogs owned by Mrs. Margrit Fischer. Ch. Ingo Wunschelrute, ROM, (top) was named Grand Victor, and Ch. Afra von Heilholtkamp, ROM, (below) became Grand Victrix. Both were important producers.

The leading ROM sire, 1967 U.S. and Can. Grand Victor, Ch. Lance of Fran-Jo, ROM, sire of 60 champions. Owned by Joan and Francis Ford.

Axel vd Deininghauserheide SchH III, DFH, FH

GV Ch Troll v Richterbach SchH III, FH

Lende v Richterbach SchH III

Ch Fortune of Arbywood ROM

Ch Cito vd Hermannschleuse

Frigga of Silver Lane ROM

Ch Jewel of Judex

1967 U.S. and CAN. Grand Victor CH. LANCE OF FRAN-JO, ROM—sire of 60 champions

GV Ch Bill v Kleistweg ROM

CH Rikter v Liebestraum

Sigga v Liebestraum

Frohlich's Elsa v Grunestahl ROM

Harold v Schlehenbusche

Burgunda v Lindendorf

Ch Ylerta v Liebestraum

Register of Merit Sires and Dams

In the early 1950s, as an aid to breeders, the German Shepherd Dog Club of America established a Register of Merit to recognize and honor the outstanding producers of the breed.

For a sire to earn ROM designation, ten or more of his progeny must earn 100 points (in accordance with a schedule set up by the parent club) and five of them must achieve AKC championship or ROM designation. For a dam the point requirement is 40, earned by four or more progeny, and two of the progeny must achieve AKC championship or ROM designation.

The point schedule has been amended through the years. At this writing (in 1981) it reads:

	3-pt. shows	4-pt. shows	5-pt. shows
BOB or BOS from Specials	6	8	10
BOB or BOS from Classes	3	4	5
Winners Dog and Winners Bitch	3	4	5
Reserve Winners Dog or Bitch	1	2	3

Dog (either sex) making championship . . . . 10 pts.
Select ratings at the National . . . . 10 pts.
ROM progeny . . . . 15 pts.
Grand Victor and Grand Victrix . . . . 15 pts.
Best in and Best Opposite at Regional Futurity . . . . 3 pts.
Best in and Best Opposite Regional Maturity . . . . 4 pts.
Best in National Futurity or Maturity . . . . 5 pts.
Best Opposite in National Futurity or Maturity . . . . 5 pts.

Canadian shows with a proven entry of 100 or more German Shepherd Dogs shown, Alaska, Hawaii and Puerto Rico shows are included in the ROM point system.

Register of Merit points are awarded for Obedience titles, too, provided that the progeny has won at least a Reserve ribbon in conformation at a major show. The schedule for Obedience points reads:

Dog, either sex, making CD title . . . . 5 pts.
Dog, either sex, making CDX title . . . . 10 pts.
Dog, either sex, making UD title . . . . 15 pts.
Dog, either sex, making TD title . . . . 5 pts.
O.T.Ch. title . . . . 5 pts.
Obedience Victor/Victrix at National Specialty . . . . 15 pts.

The lists of Register of Merit sires and dams are divided into two groups, active and inactive. When the points of a dog (or bitch) on the active list remain unchanged for a period of three years, he (or she) is transferred to the inactive list. Even though deceased, he (or she) will remain on the active list until the point total has become stable.

The lists are tabulated each year by the parent club. Following are the lists as they read with the 1980 report. On the pages that follow you will find pictures and pedigrees of many of these dogs. They represent only a sampling, but a choice sampling, of the dogs and bitches that have helped shape the breed in America over the last thirty years or so. In addition to these, pictures and pedigrees of ROM sires and dams will be found in the chapter featuring the Grand Victors and Grand Victrixes. Also pictured are some of the more impressive show winners of these years.

ACTIVE REGISTER OF MERIT SIRES

	Points		*Points*
GV Ch. Lance of Fran-Jo	3256	Covy's Oregano of Tucker Hill	435
GV Ch. Lakeside's Harrigan	2031	Ch. Ravenhaus' Noah	417
Ch. Eko-Lan's Paladen	1681	Ch. Dot-Wall's Vance	414
Ch. Cobert's Reno of Lakeside	1601	Ch. Fritz DeCloudt, CD	363
GV Ch. Yoncalla's Mike	1055	GV Ch. Caesar v. Carahaus	334
Zeus of Fran-Jo	936	Covy-Tucker Hill's Zinfandel	287
GV Ch. Hollamor's Judd	912	Ch. Peddacre's Uno, UD	246
GV Ch. Scorpio of Shiloh Gardens	866	Ch. Arbor's Benno	227
Ch. Tannenwald's Igor	828	Ch. Haydelhaus' Augie v. Zahnarzt	225
Ch. Doppelt-Tay's Hawkeye	720	Ch. Marty von Bid-Scono	196
Ch. Zeto of Fran-Jo	647	Ch. Von Nassau's Dayan	196
Ch. Caralon's Hein von der Lockenhein, CD	646	Ch. Beau of Fran-Jo	195
Ch. Lakeside's Gilligan's Island	644	Ch. Junger-Haus Caesar	190
GV Ch. Mannix of Fran-Jo	595	GV Ch. Tellaheide's Gallo	188
GV Ch. Langeneau's Watson	**563**	Ch. Kovaya's Judd	176
Ch. Kubistraum's Kane	527	Ch. Val-Don's Quaker	163
Ch. Doppelt-Tay's Hammer	492		

1972 Grand Victor Ch. Lakeside's Harrigan, ROM, sire of 50 champions. (By GV Ch. Lance of Fran-Jo ex Cobert's Melissa.) Owned by Von Nassau Kennels.

Ch. Eko-Lan's Paladen, ROM, pictured at 10 years, 10 months. Sire of 37 champions. Owned by Fred and Vicki Migliore.

<pre>
                                    Ch Fortune of Arbywood ROM
                      Am & Can GV Ch Lance of Fran-Jo ROM
                                    Frohlich's Elsa v Grunes Tahl ROM
             Ch Eko-Lan's Morgan ROM
                                    Ch Elwillo's Ursus
                      Eko-Lan's Gemini
                                    Eko-Lan's Ebb-Tide
CH. EKO-LAN'S PALADEN, ROM
                                    Ch Llano Estacado's Gengis ROM
                      Ch Elwillo's Ursus
                                    Elwillo's Francine
             Eko-Lan's Glory ROM
                                    Ch Eko-Lan's CDX
                      Eko-Lan's Ebb-Tide
                                    Eko-Lan's Anna Karinina
</pre>

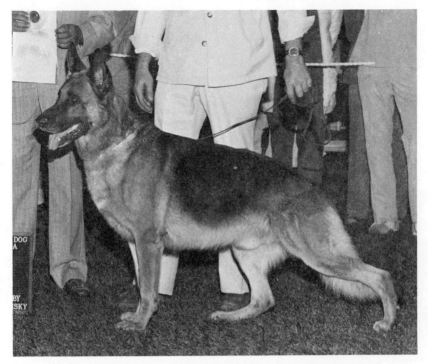

Ch. Cobert's Reno of Lakeside, ROM. Sire of 43 champions.
Owned by Vito Moreno and Connie Beckhardt.

<pre>
                        GV Ch Troll vom Richterbach ROM
            Ch Fortune of Arbywood ROM
                        Frigga of Silver Lane ROM
    Am & Can GV Ch Lance of Fran-Jo ROM
                        Ch Rikter vom Liebestraum
            Frohlich's Elsa vom Grunes Tahl ROM
                        Burgunda v Lindendorf
CH. COBERT'S RENO OF LAKESIDE, ROM
                        Ch Bernd vom Kallengarten ROM
            Ch Falk of Bihari Wonder
                        Agnes Gold of Bihari Wonder
    Cobert's Melissa ROM
                        Ch Bernd vom Kallengarten ROM
            Ch Cobert's Ernestine CD
                        Ch Cobert's Amber
</pre>

Canadian Grand Victor, Am. & Can. Ch. Ulk Wikingerblut, SchH III, AD, CACIB, ROM (1956-1968). One of the top Register of Merit point earners, he sired 46 champions including a U.S. Grand Victrix and 9 Best in Show winners. Owned by Ralph S. and Mary Roberts.

Immo v Hasenfang SchH III

Axel vd Deininghauserheide SchH III DPH FH

Helma v Hildegardsheim SchH III

Ch Troll v Richterbach SchH III FH ROM

Fels v Vogtlandshof SchH III

Lende v Richterbach SchH III

Rosel v Osnabrueckerland SchH III

CH. ULK WIKINGERBLUT SchH III AD ROM

Drusus zu den Sieben-Faulen SchH III

Ch Amor v Haus Hoheide SchH III

Christel v Fredeholz SchH Ii

Natja Wikingerblut SchH II

Rolf v Osnabrueckerland SchH III FH

Moni v Stuveschacht SchH I

Quote v Stuveschacht SchH I

INACTIVE REGISTER OF MERIT SIRES

	Points		Points
h. Ulk Wikingerblut	2222	Ch. Philberlyn's Iphiis	285
V Ch. Troll v. Richterbach	2035	Ch. Hussar of Maur-ray	282½
h. Bernd vom Kallengarten	1375	Ch. Cito v. Haus Tippersruh, UDT	260½
h. Vol of Long-Worth	1126	Ch. Seahurst Count	256
h. Nordraak of Matterhorn	905	Judd vom Liebestraum	245
h. Wotan v. Richterbach, CDX	901	Ch. Uncus of Long-Worth	245
h. Field Marshal of Arbywood	819	GV Ch. Axel v. Polidhaus	243
h. Falko von Celler Schloss	780	GV Ch. Nox of Ruthland	240
h. Fortune of Arbywood	734	Ch. San Miguel's Baron of Afbor, UD	240½
V Ch. Ingo Wunschelrut	733	Ch. Royal Rogue of Long-Worth, CD	222½
h. Gallant of Arbywood	716	Ch. Hilgrove's Emo	222
h. Chimney Sweep of Long-Worth, CD	665	Ch. Zarek v. Liebestraum	220
h. Vox Wikingerblut	644	Ch. Caesar v.d. Malmannsheide	219
V Ch. Alert of Mi-Noah	636	GV Ch. Condor v. Stoerstrudel	219
Iodo aus der Eremitenklaus	635	Hein v. Richterbach	215
h. Llano Estacado's Gengis	631	Ch. San Miguel's Ilo of Rocky Reach	210
h. Santana's Man O'War	600	Volker v. Zollgrentzschutzhaus	209
h. Eko-Lan's Morgan	593	Ch. Bodo vom Lierberg	200
h. Wilva-Don's Faust	519	Ch. Kurt v. Bid-Scono	195
h. Bismarck v. Graustein	515	Ch. Asslan of Robinsway	191
h. Harry vom Donaukai	515	Ch. Dipadon's Dasher	190
h. Jolly Arno of Edgetowne, CDX	474	Ch. Cavalier of Rocky Reach, CD	187½
V Ch. Red Rock's Gino, CD	463	GV Ch. Jory of Edgetowne, CD	186½
V Ch. Pfeffer v. Bern	460	Ch. San Miguel's Imp of Rocky Reach	182
h. Falk v. Eningsfeld	454	GV Ch. Valiant of Draham, CD	175
h. Hessian's Baldur	422	Ch. Cosalta's Ace of Wyliewood, CDX	174½
V Ch. Bill v. Kleistweg	418	Ch. Bar v. Weiherturchen	170
h. Stormhaven's Dolf	401	Ch. Ray-Mor's Fleet O' Way	161
h. Schaferhaus Vingo	398	Ch. Ex v.d. Schlangenspitze	138
h. Cuno v.d. Teufelslache	386½	Ch. Derry of Long-Worth	136
h. Quell v. Fredeholz	383	Ch. Fels v.d. Rottembrucke of Dornwald	131
rry v. Burghalderring	382	Ch. Pilot of the Wold	128½
h. Frack v.d. Burg Arkenstede	360	Ch. Mercurio of Long-Worth	121
h. Treu vom Wolfsstock	359	Ch. Merrilea's Vetter of Dornwald, CD	120
h. Fels of Arbywood	332	Odin v. Busecker Schloss	120
h. Gernda's Ludwig	307½	Ch. Marlo of Hoheluft	115
h. Doppelt-Tay's Jesse James	297	Ch. Orex of Rocky Reach, CD	110
V Ch. Yorkdom's Pak	296	Ch. Critic of Kola-Marc, CD	107
h. Wilva Don's Nordic	292	Ch. Jeffrey of Browvale	100
h. Lido v. Johanneshauch	290	Ch. Tasso of Villa Marlena	100
h. Garry of Benlore	285		

Ch. Bernd vom Kallengarten, an important influence for good in the breed.
Sire of 31 champions. Owned by Ernest Loeb.

Immo v Hasenfang
Axel vd Deininghauserheide
Helme v Hildegardsheim
Watzer v Bad Melle
Rolf v Osnabrueckerland
Imme v Bad Melle
Bette v Haus Herberhold
CH. BERND v KALLENGARTEN, ROM
Iran vd Buchenhohe
Kuno v Jungfernsprung
Bella v Haus Weinberg
Carin vd Rassweilermuhle
Lesko aus Kattenstroth
Corra vd Silverweide
Bioka vd Silverweide

60

1957 U.S. Grand Victor, 1956 Holland Grand Victor, Ch. Troll vom Richterbach, SchH III, FH, ROM, a sire whose impact has been tremendous. Owned by Irving Appelbaum. Troll is pictured with the world-famous Von Stephanitz trophy (left), awarded to the Best of Breed (Grand Victor) and the Best of Opposite Sex (Grand Victrix) at the annual specialty of the German Shepherd Dog Club of America.

Nestor v Wiegerfelsen SchH III

Immo v Hasenfang SchH III

Dorte v Hasenfang SchH I

Axel vd Deininghauserheide SchH III, DFH, FH

Gnom v Kalsmunttor SchH III

Helma vom Hildergardsheim SchH III

Tita vd Starrenburg SchH II

1957 Grand Victor CH. TROLL vom RICHTERBACH, SchH III, FH, ROM

Claudius v Hain SchH II

Fels v Vogtlandshof SchH III

Barbel v Haus Trippe SchH I

Lende v Richterbach SchH III

Lex Preussenblut SchH III

Rosel v Osnabruckerland SchH I

Maja v Osnabruckerland SchH III

Three males of the famous Arbywood "F" litter of six champions—Ch. Fels, Ch. Fortune and Ch. Field Marshal, CD. All three became strong Register of Merit sires. Owned by Mr. and Mrs. Ronald Woodard.

```
                              Immo v Hasenfang SchH III
                    Axel vd Deininghauserheide SchH III DPH FH
                         Helma v Hildegardsheim SchH III
          Ch Troll v Richterbach SchH III FH ROM
                         Fels v Vogtlandshof SchH III
             Lende v Richterbach SchH III
                         Rosel v Osnabrueckerland SchH I
ARBYWOOD "F" LITTER of 6 champions
                         Ajax v Stieg-Anger SchH III
             Ch Cito vd Herrmannschleuse
                         Hanna v Equord SchH II
          Frigga of Silver Lane ROM
                         Ch Dex of Parrylin UD
             Ch Jewel of Judex
                         Judith of Blassmor
```

Frigga of Silver Lane, ROM, dam of the Arbywood "F" litter of six champions. One of the top five in the all-time list of ROM Dams. Owned by Mr. and Mrs. Ronald Woodard.

Ch. Jewel of Judex, granddam of the Arbywood "F" litter of six champions. Owned by Clarence Alexander.

Ch. Jolly Arno of Edgetowne, CDX, ROM, a littermate of 1951 Grand Victor Ch. Jory of Edgetowne, CD. Arno was owned by Margaret Pooley's Rocky Reach Kennels.

<pre>
                                  Ch Marlo v Hoheluft ROM
                     Ch Derry of Long-Worth ROM
                                  Ch Nyx of Long-Worth ROM
            Ch Vol of Long-Worth ROM
                                  Ch Pfeffer v Bern ROM
                     Ch Ophelia of Greenfair ROM
                                  Ch Lucie v Drei-Kronen
CH. JOLLY ARNO OF EDGETOWNE, CDX, ROM
and
1951 Grand Victor CH. JORY OF EDGETOWNE, ROM
                                  Ch Marlo v Hoheluft ROM
                     Ch Derry of Long-Worth ROM
                                  Ch Nyx of Long-Worth ROM
            Ch Orpha of Edgetowne, Hon ROM
                                  Ch San Miguel's Ilo of Rocky Reach ROM
                     Bonita of Gretana
                                  Tatja v Hoheluft
</pre>

Ch. Nordraak of Matterhorn, ROM, a tremendous breeding influence on the West Coast. Owned by Helen and Harry Polonitza. Nordraak was by 1951 Grand Victor Ch. Jory of Edgetowne, CD, ex Charm of Dornwald II.

Canadian Grand Victor, Am. & Can. Ch. Chimney Sweep of Long-Worth, CD, ROM, one of the nation's top show dogs of the early '50s and sire of many champions. Owned by Virginia McCoy.

Am. & Can. Ch. Eko-Lan's Morgan, ROM.
Owned by Fred Migliore and Joseph Komma.

Ch. Vox Wikingerblut, ROM. A Best in Show winner and sire of 12 champions, two of which were Best in show winners. Owned by Ralph S. and Mary Roberts.

Ch. Hessian's Baldur, ROM, Select 1963.
Owned by Art and Helen Hess.

Arry vd Gassenquelle
Grimm vd Fahrmuhle
Fella vd Fahrmuhle
Ch. Atlas v Elfenhain
Rolf v Osnabrueckerland
Lexa v Osnabrueckerland
Vena v Osnabrueckerland
CH. HESSIAN'S BALDUR, ROM
Pirol vd Buchenhohne
Ch Quell v Fredeholz ROM
Nixie v Fredeholz
Ch Kern Delta's Exakta ROM
GV Ch Alert of Mi-Noah's ROM
Ch Gale of Stevens Rancho ROM
Ch Storm of Stevens Rancho

67

Ch. Santana's Man O' War, ROM, a top echelon sire.
Owned by Barbara Lee Williams.

Ch. Harry vom Donauki, ROM, sire of the 1959 and 1960 German Sieger Volker v.
Zollgrentzschutzhaus, ROM. Harry was owned by William S. Ford, Jr.

Ch. Bismark v. Graustein, ROM, one of the Graustein "B" litter that has been so influential on West Coast breeding. Owned by Court E. and Cale Cowley.

```
                              Ch. Vol of Long-Worth
                Ch. Jory of Edgetowne
                              Orpha of Edgetowne
        Ch. Nordraak of Matterhorn
                              Ch. Dorn of Dornwald
                Charm of Dornwald
                              Ch. Sappho of Dornwald
GRAUSTEIN "B" LITTER
                              Ch. Vol of Long-Worth
                Ch. Jolly Arno of Edgetowne
                              Ch. Orpha of Edgetowne
        Ch. Ulla of Rocky Reach
                              Ch. Baron of Rocky Reach
                Ch. Moritza of Rocky Reach
                              Riva of Rocky Reach
```

Ch. Treu vom Wolfsstock, SchH III, ROM.
Owned by Ernest Loeb.

Munko von der Hohen Fichte SchH III
Bar vom Haus Carbo SchH III
Buche vom Degenfeld SchH III
Mix von Lochem SchH I
Chico Preussenblut SchH III
Kuna von Colonial Agrippina SchH III FH
Briska von Colonial Agrippina
CH. TREU vom WOLFSSTOCK SchH III ROM
Ch Lido vom Friedlichenheim SchH III
Ex aus der Gerhardtstrasse SchH II
Gunda vom Wilischtal SchH I
Lilly vom Gipsbergwerk
Ch Armin vom Salon SchH III
Karin vom Gipsbergwerk SchH I
Manda vom Wolfsstock SchH I

Ch. Cuno v.d. Teufelslache, SchH III, ROM.
Owned by Helen Miller Fisher.

Ch. Gernda's Ludwig, ROM, whelped 1948. A Best in Show winner.
Owned by Mr. and Mrs. Robert M. Stoddard.

71

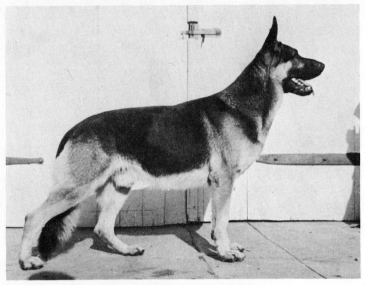

Ch. Hussar of Maur-Ray, ROM, owned by
Jean MacLatchie Borgstedt, Penllyn Kennels.

                       Sgr GV Ch Pfeffer v Bern
              GV Ch Nox of Ruthland
                       Carol of Ruthland
       Ch Viking v Hoheluft
                       Sgr GV Ch Pfeffer v Bern
              GV Ch Lady of Ruthland
                       GV Ch Frigga v Kannerbackerland
CH. HUSSAR of MAUR-RAY, ROM
                       Sgr GV Ch Pfeffer v Bern
              GV Noble of Ruthland
                       Carol of Ruthland
       Ch Leda of Ireton
                       Ch Brando v Heidelbeerberg
              Donna of Ireton
                       Rita of Ireton

Ch. Lido von Johanneshauch, ROM, important German import,
owned by Yorkdom Kennels.

1967 German Sieger, Ch. Bodo vom Lierberg, ROM,
owned by Erich Renner.

Ch. Ex. v.d. Schlangenspitze, ROM, imported by Ernest Loeb.

Condor vom Hohenstamm SchH III FH
Mutz aus der Kuckstrasse SchH III
Mori vom Gieser Waldchen SchH I
Gundo vom Preubentor SchH II
Gero vom Katharinentor SchH III FH
Poesie vom Elbbachtal SchH I
Tita von Equord SchH I
CH. EX. von der SCHLANGENSPITZE, ROM
Jalk vom Fohlenbrunnen SchH III
Lido von der Wienerau SchH III
Dixie von der Wienerau SchH I
Ossi von Erstenwald SchH I
Manno vom Stuveschacht SchH III
Nixe vom Erstenwald SchH II
Kaya vom Erstenwald SchH I

Am. & Can. Ch. Zarek v. Liebestraum, ROM,
bred and owned by Mr. & Mrs. Grant Mann.

Ch. Garry of Benlore, ROM, (1940-1948), sire of many champions in the U.S. and
Canada, including two Grand Victrixes, Leda v. Liebestraum and Jola v. Lie-
bestraum. Grandsire through Nyx of the outstanding "D" litter of Long-Worth.
Garry was owned by Mr. and Mrs. George F. Bennett.

Ch. Bar v. Weiherturchen, ROM, famed as the "Bear" dog, one of the breed's all-time great winners with a record of 12 Bests in Show, 46 Group Firsts and 107 Bests of Breed. Owned by Barbara and John Schermerhorn, and shown by Denise Kodner, now a judge. Bar was one of the many outstanding German imports brought to America by Ernest Loeb.

Ch. San Miguel's Imp of Rocky Reach, UD, ROM. Owned by Margaret Pooley.

Ch. Cosalta's Ace of Wyliewood, CD, ROM, an important East Coast breeding influence of his time. Owned by Marie J. Leary.

Pfeffer v Saliba

Pfeffer v Karinhof

Elfe v Irmendorf

Erich of Bar-Orch

Jiggs v Bar-Orch

Tippie v Bar-Orch

Vilma v Bar-Orch

CH. COSALTA'S ACE OF WYLIEWOOD, CD, ROM

Ch Bodo v Siekerfeld

Ch Giralda's Denis, CD

Giralda's Zaida

Anne of Nelgerstan

Ch Giralda's Falko CD

Frenda of Shereston

Abigail II of Shereston

Four generations of San Miguel champions (around 1950) with Obedience degrees. From left to right: Ch. Arno of San Miguel, CDX; Arno's son, Ch. San Miguel's Ilo of Rocky Reach, CDX; Ilo's son, Ch. San Miguel's Baron of Afbor, CD; and Baron's son, Ch. San Miguel's Kip of Rocky Reach, CD.

                         Ch Chlodulf v Pelztierhof PH Zpr SchH

               Ch Arno of San Miguel CDX

                    Ch Ramona of Cosalta

      Ch San Miguel's Ilo of Rocky Reach UD

                      Ch Odin v Busecker-Schloss PH

             Ch Franza of Rocky Reach CD

                  Davida of Rocky Reach

CH. SAN MIGUEL'S CHULA OF AFBOR CD

                      Tillar v Haus Hodes

               Ch Colonel v Haus Hodes

                    Blackie v Berge

          Afra of Pangamor

                      Dux v Haus Schutting

             Ch Christel v Scholerskamp SchH

                    Elsa Drei Eicheln

A representative San Miguel pedigree.

Ch. Merrilea's Vetter of Dornwald, CD, ROM, a son of Pfeffer v. Bern, and a noted winner and sire in his own right. Owned by Mr. and Mrs. James A. Cole.

Ch. Fels v.d. Rottembruecke of Dornwald, ROM, pictured in Central Park, New York City, in 1968. Fels, an import, was also owned by Mr. and Mrs. Cole.
—photo *Larry Eddington*

Ch. Gwynllan's Jeffrey of Browvale, ROM, owned by Gwynllan Kennels. Sire of the 1947 Grand Victor Ch. Dorian v. Beckgold.

Ch. Harald vom Haus Tigges, SchH III, FH, owned by Erich Renner.

Ch. Nyx of Long-Worth and three of the famous six champion "D" litter Ch. Drum, Ch. Derry (an ROM sire) and Ch. Dennis—all of Long-Worth.

Ch. Conde del Llano Estacado, owned by Langdon Skarda, today one of the nation's all-rounder judges.

7 times Select (a world record!), U.S. Maturity Victrix, Ch Tucker Hill's Angelique, CD, ROM, pictured going Select in 1977. Co-owned by Cappy Pottle, Gloria Birch and Jean Stevens.

Arno vom Haus Gersie SchH III FH

Valet vom Busecker-Schloss SchH III

Darja vom Bernstein-Strand SchH III

Holland Sgr Gauss vom Stauderpark SchH III AD

Blitz vom Mainsieg SchH III FH

Itti vom Stober Hay SchH I

Gitta vom Schloss Grimberg SchH III FH

7 times Select, U.S. Maturity Victrix

CH. TUCKER HILL'S ANGELIQUE, CD, ROM, OFA

Mix vom Lochem SchH II

Ch Treu vom Wolfsstock SchH III AD ROM

Lilly vom Gipsbergwerk SchH II

Jodi of Tucker Hill

South Am Ch Arko vom Gasthouse Rose

Golden Gwen of Tucker Hill CD

Amber N Gold of Tucker Hill CD

ACTIVE REGISTER OF MERIT DAMS

	Points		Points
Cobert's Melissa	745	GV Ch. Covy's Rosemary of Tucker Hill	105
Ch. Covy-Tucker Hill's Angelique CD	408	Fran-Jo's Dawn of Gan Edan	102
Arnhild's Black Frost	396	Kristie of Waldesruh	100
Ch. Amber's Flair	279	Doppelt-Tay's Legal Tender	99
Just A Joy of Billo	270	GV Ch. Cathwar's Lisa von Rob	97
Langenau's Quessa	260	Ch. Mirheim's Abbey	96
Ch. Kovaya's Contessa CD	256	Ch. Cobert's Golly Gee of Lakeside	95
Ch. Ponca Hill's Sudana	173	Barithaus' Ramblin' Rose	88
Ellyn Hill's Diamond Flush	166	Johnsondale's True Luv	87
Tessandra of Maplewild Hill CD	163	Wonderland's Anna of Cave Hill	86
Yoncalla's Patti of Sunny Bee	161	Eko-Lan's Rhyme	80
Ch. Amber's Valiant Robin	151	Ch. Covy's Felita of Tucker Hill	79
Del-Deena of Waldesruh	151	Kenwood's Clove of Bay Meadow	73
Gracelyn's Gay Blade	146	Smoketree's Americana	71
GV Ch. Aloaha of Bid-Scono	135	Kismet's Deliah	69
Ch. Cobert's Windsong	132	Cobert's Rhythm of Lakeside	68
Von Auckland's Melody Rocket	128	GV Ch. Lor-Locke's Tatta's of Fran-Jo	66
Ch. Elfie of Fran-Jo	127	Ch. Kovaya's Jill CD	63
Jill of Seebree	121	Echowood's Raquel of Louron	60
Ch. Lakeside's Just Jamaica	121	Glenhart's Della of Ayrwood	58
Ch. Covy's Tartar of Tucker Hill	109	Edelheim's Bianka Tulpenheim	57
Ch. Von Nassau's Galaxie CD	108	Kovaya's Amanda of Shadowbrook	56
Samian's Image	106		

Ch. Cobert's Golly Gee of Lakeside, ROM, litter sister to Ch. Lakeside's Gilligan's Island. Owned by the Beckhardts.

INACTIVE REGISTER OF MERIT DAMS

HONORARY ROM DAMS

Ch. Long-Worth's Ophelia
Dornwald's Klodette v. Bar-Orch
Ch. Winnette of Long-Worth
Ch. Orpha of Edgetowne
Ch. Eroica of Dornwald
Elga of Long-Worth
Ch. Sappho of Dornwald
Ch. Franza of Rocky Reach
Ramona of Cosalta
Ch. Vicki v. Hoheluft
Elga v. Saliba

	Points		Point
Frohlich's Elsa v. Grunes Tahl	551	Belgrade's Roquette.	25
Sacha Wikingerblut	512	Ch. Wilva Don's Sonnig v. Thornoaks	25
Frigga of Silver Lane	511	Ch. Nether-Lair's Gaitey.	23
Ch. Ulla of Rocky Reach II	453	Ch. Victoria of the Harrisons	21
Robin of Nikral	373	Ch. Asta vom Haus Bernius	20
Ch. Val-Koa's Kellee	372	Frolic of Clover Acres	19
Ch. Wilva Don's Schatz v. Thornoaks	310	Chickwood's Gillie	18
GV Ch. Bonnie Bergere of Ken Rose UDT	308	Ch. Llana Estacado's Cece	18
Ch. Copper Canyon's Intrique CD	304	Hy-Verta's Brunhilda of Woodacres	18
Hessian's Quella	288	Ch. Gale of Steven's Rancho CDX	16
Frigga of Mill Lake Farm	287	Ch. Hy-Verta's Candy	16
Ch. Von Schrief's Portrait	287	Von Leebrin's Debutante	16
Hillgrove's Erle.	267	Ch. Ricella's Fantasy	16
Kanna of Rocky Reach	257	Von Nassau's Ophelia	16
Ch. Ginger Girl of Long-Worth	254	Wilva Don's Leda	15
Von Nassau's Schemaine.	252	Carol of Ruthland	15

Honorary ROM Dam, Ch. Sappho of Dornwald, owned by Mr. and Mrs. James A. Cole's famous Dornwald Kennels.

Honorary ROM Dam, Ch. Franza of Rocky Reach, owned by Margaret Pooley.

	Points
Eko-Lan's Glory	147
Tiedel's Patti CD	147
Hulla v. Sieghaus	144
Curta of Friendship Acres	141
Wilhelm's Rita of Rocoway CDX	139
Freia v. Wiekau	136
Bess of Wynthea	132
Ch. Chickwood's Feather	125
GV Ch. Frigga v. Hoheluft	125
Ch. Kara v. Kuperhof	125
Zaida v. Liebestraum	125
Jeff-Lynn's Black Magic	119
Edenvale's Nita	117
Philberlyn's Ilsa	114
Wingait's Becky	112
Von Nassau's Mindy	111
Ch. Judy of San Miguel CD	110
Ch. Jola von Liebestraum	110
Tannenburg Lady Hulda	109
Ch. Kern Delta's Exakta	108
Ch. Tanya of Rocky Reach CD	107
Ch. Copper Canyon's Nita	106
Lou-Ed's Carus	106
Wilda Wikingerblut	106
Sheena of Delray	106
Ch. Gail of Penllyn	104
Ch. Wilva Don's Barda	103
Ch. Oricka of Rocky Reach	102
Briska v.d. Burg Kendenich	101
Major's Debbie	101
Aurora of Scotmar	100
Ch. Galewynd's Christine	98
Schaferhaus Fenya	98
Ch. Amber aus der Edelheim	96
Ch. San Miguel's Chula of Arbor CD	95
GV Ch. Hessian's Vogue	93
Reinzucht's Sunbeam	93
Lahngold's Admiration	92
Den-Lea's High Jinx CD	91
Ch. Kandy of Delray	90
Von Nassu's Gesha	90
Ch. Lonie of Fran-Jo	89
Ch. Cassy of Waldesruh	88
Ch. Bru-Star's Yore Lore	87
Trulander's Celebrity	86

	Points
Ch. Christel of San Miguel CD	85
Nether-Lair's Helena	83
Amber's Regina	83
Ch. Moritza of Rocky Reach	82
Starlight of Cosalta	80
Vonda v. Liebestraum	80
Sin's Aint Miss Behavin	79
Ch. Willow Grange Dark Angel	79
Kathy of Mi-Noah's	77
Waldenmark's Levade Preusenblut	76
Aeromist of Long-Worth	74
Ch. Debbie of Knollcrest	74
Ch. Rin's Elana of River Edge	74
GV Ch. Sola Nina of Rushagen CD	72
Von Nassau's Delight	69
Nanhall's Julip	69
Caret vom Elfenhaim	68
Ch. Minka of Hobby House	68
Dina of Waldesruh	65
GV Ch. Afra v. Heilholtkamp	61
Elfi of Jo-Mar	61
Bel-Vista's La Negra Onyx	60
Evida of Grafmar	60
Flame of San Miguel	60
Ch. Llana Estacado's Tina	60
Lorren's Asta	60
Santana's Miss Barb Cat	60
Bee Jay's Holiday of Gan Edan	59
Amber's DeCloudt's Cristl	55
Von Nordland's Diedre of Maji CD	55
Granada's Echo	52
Ch. Afra v. Wormser-Weg	50
Ch. Abigail of Shereston II	50
Autumn of Seamair	50
GV Ch. Leda v. Liebestraum	50
Hessian's Robina	50
Ch. Ophelia of Greenfair	45
San Miguel's Bria v. Huenhoert CD	45
Ch. Seahurst Bonita	43
Walda of Long-Worth	40
Griselda of Long-Worth	40
Abigail v. Waldeslust	40
Ch. Lolly of Dornwald	40
Ch. Firelei of Dornwald	40

Ch. Ulla of Rocky Reach II, ROM, one of the all-time tops in ROM points. Owned by Court and Cale Cowley.

Ch. Von Schrief's Portrait, ROM, a top winning bitch of the late 1950s. Owned by Mr. and Mrs. Doyle A. Williams.

Ch. Kara v. Kuperhof, ROM, by Ch. Jolly Arno of Edgetowne, CDX, ROM ex Ch. Oricka of Rocky Reach, CD, ROM. Owned by Margaret Pooley, Rocky Reach Kennels.

Ch. Lanna v. Kuperhof, owned by B.H. Kuper.

Ch. Kern Delta's Exacta, ROM, a daughter of Ch. Quell v. Fredeholz, owned by Art and Helen Hess's Hessian Kennels.

Ch. Cobert's Ernestine, CD, an oustanding Bernd v. Kallengarten daughter. Owned by Mr. and Mrs. Theodore Beckhardt.

Ch. Von Der Ley Rhinestone Cowboy, scoring at the 1980 Specialty.
Owner, Luis M. Colarte.

<pre>
                         Am & Can GV Ch Lance of Fran-Jo ROM
             Ch Lakeside's Gilligan's Island
                         Cobert's Melissa ROM
      Am & Can Ch Von der Ley's Midnight Cowboy
                         Ch Imperial von Celler Schloss
             Von Trenkner's Caliente CD
                         Ch Hatari von Celler Schloss
CH. VON DER LEY'S RHINESTONE COWBOY
                         Ch Eko-Lan's Morgan ROM
             Ch Eko-Lan's Quasar
                         Eko-Lan's Loner
      Galewynd's Channacha
                         Ch Robinsway Heiko
             Galewynd's Sonata
                         Galewynd's Ilisa
</pre>

Am. & Can. Ch. Bihari's Klodo, UD, 1974-1975 American Select, 1975 Canadian Select. Klodo has received the Quaker Oats Hero medal—once saving his master from a car fire, and another time he ran for assistance when his mistress fell down the stairs and was badly injured. Owned by Herbert and Chris Merkel.

Am & Can GV Ch Lance of Fran-Jo ROM

Ch Eko-Lan's Morgan ROM

Eko-Lan's Gemini ROM

Ch Eko-Lan's Paladen ROM

Ch Elwillo's Ursus

Eko-Lan's Glory ROM

Eko-Lan's Ebb-Tide

AM. & CAN. CH. BIHARI'S KLODO, CDX, UD

Jalk vom Fohlenbrunnen SchH III

Black vom Lambertzeck SchH II

Ulla vom Glockenland SchH III

Helma von der Sturmwolke SchH IIa

Fix zu den Sieben Faulen SchH III

Romy von der Sturmwolke SchH II

Otti vom Steckkenborn SchH II

Ch. Holiday's Kheigh Deigh, 1976 National Futurity Victor.
Bred and owned by Judy Johnson.

                                  GV Ch Brix v Grafenkrone
                        Kerry of Waldesruh
                                  Del-Dena of Waldesruh
            Ch Ravenhaus Noah ROM
                                  Ch Cappilway's Dotan
                        Can Ch Ravenhaus Ganiff
                                  Ravenhaus Extacy
CH. HOLIDAY'S KHEIGH DEIGH
                                  GV Ch Yoncalla's Mike ROM
                        GV Ch Hollamor's Judd
                                  Franchon of Edgetowne
            Nocturne's Fire Fly Girl
                                  GV Ch Condor v Stoerstrudel ROM
                        Gorlin's Cassandra
                                  Nanhall's Julip ROM

Ch. Bel Vista's Joey Baby, a 1970's star.

<pre>
                              Ch Fortune of Arbywood ROM
                  GV Am & Can Ch Lance of Fran-Jo ROM
                              Frohlich's Elsa v Grunestahl ROM
        Bel Vista's Loredo
                              GV Ch Yoncallas Mike ROM
                  Bel Vista's Beau Hannah
                              Bel Vista's La Negra Onyx
CH. BEL VISTA'S JOEY BABY
                              Ch Caralons Hein v Lochenheim ROM
                  Ch Alemans Curt
                              Hessian's Balincia of Alemans
        Diedra v Knaffl-Hof
                              Am & Can GV Ch Lance of Fran-Jo ROM
                  Knaffl-Hof's Matilda of Epidau
                              Barda of Epidau
</pre>

Big ribbons for big wins. 1979 Grand Victor, Ch. Schokrest On Parade.
Owner, Lorraine Schowalter.

4

The Grand Victors
and Grand Victrixes—
U.S.A.

THE TITLE "Grand Victor" is bestowed upon the male winning Best of Breed or Best of Opposite Sex at the annual Specialty Show of the German Shepherd Dog Club of America, and the title "Grand Victrix" is given to the bitch winning Best of Breed or Best of Opposite Sex. In early years, until 1925, the winners were called "Grand Champion."

No awards were made in 1932 because the judge (brought over from Germany for the show) felt that there was neither a dog or bitch that was worthy of the title. Again, in 1936, a judge from Germany felt that there was no male worthy of the "Grand Victor" designation, but did select a Grand Victrix.

Because a date could not be agreed upon with the American Kennel Club, there was no Specialty Show in 1964, and hence no awards for that year.

95

1939 U.S. Grand Victor, Ch. Hugo of Cosalta, CD,
owned by Marie J. Leary.

1942 U.S. Grand Victor, Ch. Noble of Ruthland, a Ch. Pfeffer v. Bern son.
Owned by Henry J. Daube.

GRAND VICTORS

1918	Komet v. Hoheluft
1919	Apollo v. Hunenstein
1920	Rex v. Buckel
1921	Ch. Grimm v.d. Mainkur, PH
1922	Ch. Erich v. Grafenwerth, PH
1923	Ch. Dolf v. Dusternbrook, PH
1924	Ch. Cito Bergerslust, SchH
1925	Ch. Cito Bergerslust, SchH
1926	Ch. Donar v. Overstolzen, SchH
1927	Ch. Arko v. Sadowaberg, SchH
1928	Ch. Arko v. Sadowaberg, SchH
1929	Ch. Arko v. Sadowaberg, SchH
1930	Ch. Bimbo v. Stolzenfels
1931	Ch. Arko v. Sadowaberg, SchH
1932	*Not Awarded*
1933	Golf v. Hooptal
1934	Ch. Erekind of Shereston
1935	Ch. Nox of Glenmar
1936	*Not Awarded*
1937	Ch. Pfeffer v. Bern, ZPrMH, ROM
1938	Ch. Pfeffer v. Bern, ZPrMH, ROM
1939	Ch. Hugo of Cosalta, CD
1940	Ch. Cotswald of Cosalta, CD
1941	Ch. Nox of Ruthland, ROM
1942	Ch. Noble of Ruthland
1943	Major of Northmere
1944	Ch. Nox of Ruthland, ROM
1945	Ch. Adam of Veralda
1946	Dex of Talladega, CD
1947	Ch. Dorian v. Beckgold
1948	Ch. Valiant of Draham, CD, ROM
1949	Ch. Kirk of San Miguel
1950	Ch. Kirk of San Miguel
1951	Ch. Jory of Edgetowne, CD, ROM
1952	Ch. Ingo Wunschelrute, ROM
1953	Ch. Alert of Mi-Noah's, ROM
1954	Ch. Brando v. Aichtal
1955	Ch. Rasant v. Holzheimer Eichwald, SchH II
1956	Ch. Bill v. Kleistweg, ROM

1957	Ch. Troll v. Richterbach, SchH III, ROM
1958	Ch. Yasko v. Zenntal, SchH III
1959	Ch. Red Rock's Gino, CD, ROM
1960	Ch. Axel v. Poldihaus, ROM
1961	Ch. Lido v. Mellerland
1962	Ch. Yorkdom's Pak
1963	Ch. Condor v. Stoerstrudel, SchH I, ROM
1964	*No Competition*
1965	Ch. Brix v.d. Grafenkrone, SchH III, ROM
1966	Ch. Yoncalla's Mike, ROM
1967	Ch. Lance of Fran-Jo, ROM
1968	Ch. Yoncalla's Mike, ROM
1969	Ch. Arno v.d. Kurpfalzhalle, SchH III
1970	Ch. Hollamor's Judd, ROM
1971	Ch. Mannix of Fran-Jo, ROM
1972	Ch. Lakeside's Harrigan, ROM
1973	Ch. Scorpio of Shiloh Gardens, ROM
1974	Ch. Tellaheide's Gallo
1975	Ch. Caesar von Carahaus, ROM
1976	Ch. Padechma's Persuasion
1977	Ch. Langenau's Watson
1978	Ch. Baobab's Chaz
1979	Ch. Schokrest On Parade
1980	Ch. Aspen of Fran-Jo
1981	Ch. Sabra Dennis of Gan Edan

1948 U.S. Grand Victor, Am. & Can. Ch. Valiant of Draham, CD.
Owned by David McCahill.

1947 U.S. Grand Victor, Ch. Dorian von Beckgold,
bred and owned by William Goldbecker.

1949 and 1950 U.S. Grand Victor, Ch. Kirk of San Miguel.
Owned by Miss Marie J. Leary.

1951 U.S. Grand Victor, Ch. Jory of Edgetowne, CD, ROM.
Owned by Mrs. Betty Ford.

1953 U.S. Grand Victor, Ch. Alert of Mi-Noah's, ROM.
Owned by Noah Bloomer, Mi-Noah's Kennels.

Ch Arno of San Miguel CDX
Ch San Miguel's Ilo of Rocky Reach UD
Ch Franza of Rocky Reach CD
Ch San Miguel's Baron of Afbor UD
Ch Colonel v Haus Hodes CDX
Afra of Pangamor
Ch Christel v Scholarskamp SchH
1953 Grand Victor CH. ALERT OF MI-NOAH'S
Ch Odin v Busecker-Schloss PH
Alert of Long-Worth
Orla v Liebestraum
Mi-Noah's Ophelia of Long-Worth
Sgr GV Ch Pfeffer v Bern Zpr
Ch Long-Worth's Ophelia of Greenfair
Ch Lucie vd Drei-Kronen

101

1954 U.S. Grand Victor, Ch. Brando vom Aichtal.
Owner, Mrs. Marion McDermott, Sarego Kennels.

1955 Grand Victor, Ch. Rasant vom Holzheimer Eichwald, SchH II.
Owned by Frank S. Kupfer.

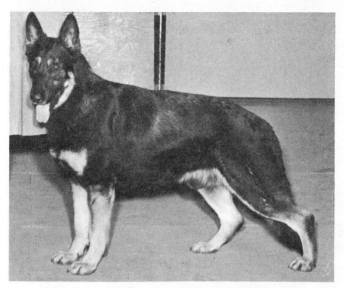

1959 U.S. Grand Victor, Ch. Red Rock's Gino, CD, ROM.
Owned by Nether-Lair Kennels.

                                        Ch Vol of Long-Worth
                     Ch Jolly Arno of Edgetowne CDX ROM
                                Ch Orpha of Edgetowne ROM
            Ch Edenvale's Nikki CD Hon ROM
                              Ch Marlo v Hoheluft ROM
                    Lois of Edgetowne
                    Donna of Edgetowne
1959 Grand Victor CH. RED ROCK'S GINO, CD, ROM
                        GV Valiant of Draham CD
                Ch Keenland of Grafmar UDT
                        Donna v Grafmar UDT
            Kay of Ayron
                        GV Ch Nox of Ruthland
                Nikki of Browvale
                        Ch Vicki v Hoheluft

1960 U.S. Grand Victor, Axel v.d. Poldihaus, ROM,
Owned by Otto Meier.

1961 U.S. Grand Victor, Ch. Lido v. Mellerland.
Owned by Ernest Loeb and Neil Gelzeiler.

1962 U.S. Grand Victor, Ch. Yorkdom's Pak, ROM.
Owned by Mrs. Polly Katz and Ted Yonemoto.

                          Kosak v Holzheimer Eichwald SchH I
           Arry v Eilsbrunn SchH III
                    Kudrun vd Natternburg SchH III
Ch Lido v Johannesbauch
                    Ch Lord v Zenntal SchH II
          Ilse v Sieghaus SchH II
                    Burga vd Marienbrucke SchH I
1962 Grand Victor CH. YORKDOM'S PAK, ROM
                    Rolf v Osnabrueckerland SchH II
          Caesar v Haus Amlung SchH III FH
                    Bianka Preussenblut Sch I
Jutta v Colonia Agrippina
                    Cuno vd Kroschburg SchH I
          Asta vd Bisheiligangrotte SchH II
                    Bella v Nassauhugel SchH I

1963 U.S. Grand Victor, Ch. Condor vom Stoerstrudel, SchH I, ROM.
Owned by Thomas L. Bennett and Fred Becker, Jr., and handled by
Lamar Kuhns.

1965 U.S. Grand Victor, Ch. v.d. Grafenkrone, SchH III.
Owned by Ernest Loeb.

1966 and 1968 U.S. Grand Victor, Ch. Yoncalla's Mike.
Owned by Mr. and Mrs. Robert Freeny.

1969 U.S. Grand Victor, Ch. Arno v.d. Kurpfalzhalle.
Owned by Sam Lawrence.

1971 U.S. Grand Victor, Ch. Mannix of Fran-Jo, ROM.
Bred and owned by J.D. and F.L. Ford, Sr.

GV Ch Troll v Richterbach ROM
Ch Fortune of Arbywood ROM
Frigga of Silver Lane ROM
GV Ch Lance of Fran-Jo ROM
Ch Rikter v Liebestraum
Frohlich's Elsa von Grunestahl ROM
Burgunda v Lindendorf
1971 Grand Victor CH. MANNIX OF FRAN-JO, ROM
Warzer v Bad Melle
Ch Bernd v Kallengarten ROM
Carin vd Rassweilermuhle
Hillgrove's Erle ROM
Ch Alf v Loherfeld
Ch Toni of Fieldstone
Freia vd Wiekau

1973 U.S. Grand Victor, Ch. Scorpio of Shiloh Gardens, ROM.
Owned by Thomas L. and Carol McPheron.

1974 U.S. Grand Victor, Ch. Tellaheide's Gallo,
Co-owned by Lucille Latella and Lee and Francine Amster.

1975 U.S. Grand Victor, Ch. Caesar von Carahaus, ROM.
Owners, Dr. and Mrs. Ralph Neal.

Ch Fortune of Arbywood ROM

Am & Can GV Ch Lance of Fran-Jo ROM

Frohlich's Elsa v Grunestahl ROM

GV Ch Mannix of Fran-Jo ROM

Ch Bernd v Kallengarten SchH II, ROM

Hillgrove's Erle ROM

Ch Toni of Fieldstone

1975 Grand Victor CH. CAESAR von CARAHAUS, ROM

Jardo's Kurt of Cosalta

Ch Tannenwald's Igor ROM

Bruni of Tannenwald

Aretha of Glentaner

GV Ch Axel vd Poldihaus ROM

Weberhaus War Ember of Fries

Hofje's Dark Victory

1977 U.S. Grand Victor Ch. Langenau's Watson.
Owners, Dave and Martha Rinke.

1978 U.S. Grand Victor, Ch. Baobab's Chaz.
Bred and Owned by George and Donna Lundy.

1980 U.S. Grand Victor, Ch. Aspen of Fran-Jo.
Breeder-Owners: Joan D. and Francis L. Ford, Sr.

                              GV Ch Mannix of Fran-Jo ROM
                     Spartacus of Shiloh Gardens
                              Waldesruh's Pud of Shiloh Gardens
           Quint of Shiloh Gardens
                              GV Ch Scorpio of Shiloh Gardens ROM
                     Trisha of Shiloh Gardens
                              Xenia of Shiloh Gardens
1980 Grand Victor CH. ASPEN OF FRAN-JO
                              Ch Eko-Lan's Morgan ROM
                     Ch Eko-Lan's Paladen ROM
                              Eko-Lan's Glory ROM
           Ch Elfie of Fran-Jo ROM
                              Ch Fortune of Arbywood ROM
                     Ch. Lonie of Fran-Jo ROM
                              Frolich's Elsa v Grunestahl ROM

1981 U.S. Grand Victor, Ch. Sabra Dennis of Gan-Eden.
Owners, Mimi and Art Saltz.

               Ch Beau of Fran-Jo ROM
         Ch. Gabriel of Gan Edan
             Bee-Jay's Holiday of Gan Edan
    Ch. Ozark of Gan Edan
             Ch. Zar Zal's Liko
        Andoro's Aria
             Ellyn Hill's Diamond Flush ROM
1981 Grand Victor CH. SABRA DENNIS OF GAN EDAN
             GV Ch Lance of Fran-Jo ROM
        Ch Zeto of Fran-Jo ROM
             Ch Mirheim's Abby ROM
    Fran-Jo's Dawn of Gan Edan ROM
             Ch. Eko-Lan's Paladen ROM
        Lonnie of Jo-Mar
             Elfie of Jo-Mar

1944 U.S. Grand Victrix, Ch. Frigga v. Hoheluft, ROM.
Owner, Bernard Daku.

1946 U.S. Grand Victrix, Ch. Leda v. Liebestraum, ROM,
Breeder-Owner, Grant Mann.

GRAND VICTRIXES

1918	Lotte v. Edelweiss
1919	Vanhall's Herta
1920	Boda v.d. Fuerstenburg
1921	Dora v. Rheinwald
1922	Debora v. Weimar
1923	Boda v.d. Fuerstenburg
1924	Irma v. Doernerhof, SchH
1925	Irma v. Doernerhof, SchH
1926	Ch. Asta v.d. Kaltenweide
1927	Ch. Inky of Willowgate
1928	Ch. Erich's Merceda of Shereston
1929	Ch. Katja v. Blaisenberg, ZPr
1930	Christel v. Stimmberg, PH
1931	Ch. Gisa v. Koenigsbruch
1932	*Not Awarded*
1933	Ch. Dora of Shereston
1934	Ch. Dora of Shereston
1935	Ch. Nanka v. Schwyn
1936	Ch. Frigga v. Kannenbaeckerland
1937	Ch. Perchta v. Bern
1938	Ch. Giralda's Geisha
1939	Ch. Thora v. Bern of Giralda
1940	Ch. Lady of Ruthland, ROM
1941	Ch. Hexe of Rotundina
1942	Ch. Bella v. Haus Hagen
1943	Ch. Bella v. Haus Hagen
1944	Ch. Frigga v. Hoheluft, ROM
1945	Ch. Olga of Ruthland
1946	Ch. Leda v. Liebestraum, ROM
1947	Ch. Jola v. Liebestraum, ROM
1948	Ch. Duchess of Browvale
1949	Doris v. Vogtlandshof
1950	Ch. Yola of Long-Worth
1951	Ch. Tawnee of Liebestraum
1952	Ch. Afra v. Heilholtkamp, ROM
1953	Ch. Ulla of San Miguel
1954	Ch. Jem of Penllyn
1955	Ch. Sola Nina of Rushagen, ROM
1956	Ch. Kobeil's Barda

1947 U.S. Grand Victrix, Ch. Jola v. Liebestraum, owned and handled by Grant Mann. Grant Mann was noted for his great showmanship. Whenever permitted, he exhibited his dogs off-lead; his handling methods were taught to many of the top handlers of the Midwest for many years.

<pre>
                                    Ch Odin v Busecker-Schloss PH
                        Falko of Benlore
                            Ch Erna of Benlore
            Ch Garry of Benlore
                            Eburt of Benlore
                Ardis of Mergenhaus
                    Quip of Garastanna
1947 Grand Victrix CH. JOLA v LIEBESTRAUM
                            Ch Rex v Liebestraum II
                Int Ch Orex v Liebestraum
                        Zaida v Liebestraum
            Norbert of Brairnole
                            Delilah v Liebestraum
                Lameg v Larro
</pre>

1948 U.S. Grand Victrix, Ch. Duchess of Browvale.
Owned by Mr. and Mrs. Gustave Schindler.

1951 U.S. Grand Victrix, Ch. Tawnee v. Liebestraum.
Owned by Grant Mann.

1955 U.S. Grand Victrix, Ch. Solo Nina of Rushagen, CD, ROM.
Owned by Mr. and Mrs. Harvey Arnold.

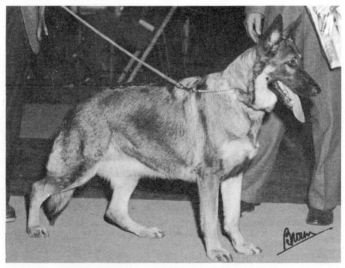

1957 U.S. Grand Victrix Ch. Jeff-Lynne's Bella.
Owned by Mr. and Mrs. Robert O'Donnell.

GRAND VICTRIXES (cont'd.)

1957   Ch. Jeff-Lynne's Bella
1958   Ch. Tan-Zar Desiree
1959   Ch. Alice v.d. Guten Fee, SchH I, ROM
1960   Ch. Robin of Kingscroft
1961   Ch. Nanhall's Donna
1962   Ch. Bonnie Bergere of Ken-Rose, UDT, ROM
1963   Ch. Hessian's Vogue, ROM
1964   *No Competition*
1965   Ch. Marsa's Velvet of Malabar
1966   Ch. Hanarob's Touche
1967   Ch. Hanarob's Touche
1968   Ch. Valtara's Image
1969   Ch. DeCloudt's Heidi, CD
1970   Ch. Bel Vista's Solid Sender
1971   Ch. Aloha v. Bid-Scono
1972   Ch. Cathwar's Lisa von Rob
1973   Ch. Ro San's First Love
1974   Ch. Lor-Locke's Tatta of Fran-Jo
1975   Ch. Langenau's Tango of Fran-Jo
1976   Ch. Covy's Rosemary of Tucker Hill, ROM
1977   Ch. Charo of Shiloh Gardens
1978   Ch. Jo-San's Charisma
1979   Ch. Anton's Jesse
1980   Ch. Lacy Britches of Billo
1981   Ch. Anton's Jenne

1963 U.S. Grand Victrix, Ch. Hessian's Vogue, ROM,
Bred and owned by Helen Hess.

                    Axel vd Deininghauserheide SchH III, DFH, FH
          GV Ch Troll v Richterbach SchH III, FH, ROM
                    Lende v Richterbach
   Ch Kurt v Bid-Scono
                    Arno v Beerbach
          Bella vd Wagnersgruben
                    Cita v Tauenwalde
1963 Grand Victrix CH. HESSIAN'S VOGUE, ROM
                    Ch Baron of Afbor ROM
          GV Ch Alert of Mi-Noah's ROM
                    Ophelia of Long-Worth
   Hessian's Quella ROM
                    Ch Quell v Fredeholz ROM
          Ch Kern Delta's Exakta ROM
                    Ch Gale of Stevens Rancho

1961 U.S. Grand Victrix, Ch. Nanhall's Donna.
Owned by Nanhall Kennels and W.P. Sanders.

1962 U.S. Grand Victrix, Ch. Bonnie Bergere of Ken-Rose, CD,
dam of the 1961 Grand Victrix, Ch. Nanhalls Donna.
Owned by Nanhall Kennels and W.P. Sanders.

1969 U.S. Grand Victrix, Ch. DeCloudt's Heidi.
Owners: Mr. and Mrs. Frank C. Cloudt.

1970 U.S. Grand Victrix, Ch. Bel Vista's Solid Sender.
Owners: Charlotte and Joe Poepping.

1971 U.S. Grand Victrix, Canadian Grand Victrix, Ch. Aloha von Bid-Scono.
Owner: Luke E. Geraghty.

1972 U.S. Grand Victrix Ch. Cathwar's Lisa von Rob.
Owners: Dr. and Mrs. Peter W. Ross, Jr.

1973 U.S. Grand Victrix, Ch. Ro San's First Love.
Owner: Carolyn Hammond.

1974 U.S. Grand Victrix, Ch. Lor-Locke's Tatta of Fran-Jo.
Owners: Joan Ford and Ralph Locke.

1976 U.S. Grand Victrix, Ch. Covy's Rosemary of Tucker Hill, ROM.
Owners: Cappy Pottle and Gloria F. Birch.

1977 U.S. Grand Victrix, Ch. Charo of Shiloh Gardens.
Owners, Thomas and Carol McPheron.

1978 U.S. Grand Victrix, Ch. Jo-San's Charisma,
1976 Maturity Victrix and Select 2.
Owner: Mrs. Sandra Abbruzzese.

                                   Ch Fortune of Arbywood ROM
                        Am & Can GV Lance of Fran-Jo ROM
                                   Frolich's Elsa vom Grunes Tahl ROM
Ch Reno of Lakeside ROM
                                   Ch Falk of Bihari Wonder
                      Cobert's Melissa ROM
                                   Ch Cobert's Ernestine CD
1978 Grand Victrix CH. JO-SAN'S CHARISMA
                                 Am & Can GV Lance of Fran-Jo ROM
                      GV CH Lakeside's Harrigan
                                 Cobert's Melissa ROM
Covy's Bonita of Tucker Hill
                                 Ch Peddacres
                      Covy's Ali of Tucker Hill
                               Kovaya's Kemi

1979 U.S. Grand Victrix, 1978 Canadian Grand Victrix,
Am. & Can. Ch. Anton's Jesse.
Owner: Joseph Bihari.

                                  Ch Fortune of Arbywood ROM
            Am & Can GV Lance of Fran-Jo ROM
                  Frohlich's Elsa v Grunes Tahl
Zeus of Fran-Jo ROM
                  Am & Can GV Ch Lance of Fran-Jo ROM
            Ch Mirheim's Abbey
                  Ch Kingsdown's Amber
1979 Grand Victrix CH. ANTON'S JESSE
                  Kerry of Waldesruh
            Arnhilds Crusader
                  Robinsway Anka
Arnhilds Black Frost ROM
                  Kerry of Waldesruh
            Arnhilds Cognac
                  Robinsway Anka

1980 U.S. Grand Victrix, Ch. Lacy Britches of Billo.
Breeders: Bill and Lois Greene, Billo Shepherds.
Owner: Johanna Smith, Sonnenwald Kennels.

                                    Ch Fortune of Arbywood ROM
                          Am & Can GV Lance of Fran-Jo ROM
                                    Frohlich's Elsa v Grunes Tahl ROM
                    Zeus of Fran-Jo ROM
                                    Am & Can GV Ch Lance of Fran-Jo ROM
                          Ch Mirheim's Abbey
                                    Can Ch Kingsdown's Amber
1980 Grand Victrix CH. LACEY BRITCHES OF BILLO
                                    Lang of Waldesruh
                          Galewynd's Trojan
                                    Galewynd's Symphony
                    Just A Joy of Billo ROM
                                    Am & Can GV Ch Lance of Fran-Jo ROM
                          Ch Maja of Wadlesruh
                                    Lil' Lulu of Waldesruh

OBEDIENCE VICTORS
and VICTRIXES

Beginning in 1968, the German Shepherd Dog Club of America established a designation to honor the dog achieving the highest combined score in the Obedience competition at the Specialty each year. If the winner is a male, he will be called "Obedience Victor," and if it is a bitch, the title will be "Obedience Victrix."

Stipulations for the award are: Highest Combined Score of a dog or bitch in Open B and Utility Classes with a combined score of at least 385, scores in each class of at least 190, and proof of having won a ribbon in conformation competition. Limitations were placed on this award to exclude animals with disqualifying faults of conformation.

In the inaugural year, Heidi Von Zook, UDT, owner-trained-handled by Ron Roberts, became the first Obedience Victrix.

1968   Heide Von Sook, UDT
1970   Schillenkamp Duke of Orleans, UDT
1971   Bihari's Uncle Sam, UD
1972   Ruglor's Reboza Von Zook, UD
1973   Brunhild of Ravenna, UDT, SchH I
1974   Kelnorth Lady Jessica, UDT
1975   Penny Auf Der Heide, UDT
1976   Natasha Von Hammhausen, UD
1977   Herta Von Hammhausen, UD
1978   Indra Von Hoheneichen, UD
1979   O.T.Ch. Johnsondale's Kool Kaper, UD
1980   O.T.Ch. Von Jenin's Link, TD
1981   *Not Awarded*

1974 Obedience Victrix, Kenilworth Lady Jessica, UDT.

1976 Obedience Victrix, Natasha von Hammhausen, UD.

1977 Obedience Victrix, Herta von Hammhausen, UD.

1979 Obedience Victrix,
O.T. Ch. Johnsondale's Kool Kaper, UD.

An all-time top winner of the breed, Am. & Can. Ch. Val-Koa's Roon, winner of 203 Bests of Breed, 110 Working Group Firsts and 30 Bests in Show. By Ch. Vox Wikingerblut, ROM ex Sel. Ch. Val-Koa's Kellee, ROM, Roon was the Quaker Oats Award winner (for most Group wins—all breeds) in 1974. Bred by Mary Roberts and Joseph Totora, owned by Mary Roberts (handling him here) and G. W. Anderson, M.D.

5

Official Breed Standard of the German Shepherd Dog

Submitted by the German Shepherd Dog Club of America, and approved by the American Kennel Club, April 9, 1968, with additions approved February 11, 1978.

General Appearance—The first impression of a good German Shepherd Dog is that of a strong, agile, well-muscled animal, alert and full of life. It is well balanced, with harmonious development of the forequarter and hindquarter. The dog is longer than tall, deep-bodied, and presents an outline of smooth curves rather than angles. It looks substantial and not spindly, giving the impression, both at rest and in motion, of muscular fitness and nimbleness without any look of clumsiness or soft living. The ideal dog is stamped with a look of quality and nobility—difficult to define, but unmistakable when present. Secondary sex characteristics are strongly marked, and every animal gives a definite impression of masculinity or femininity, according to its sex.

Character—The breed has a distinct personality marked by direct and fearless, but not hostile, expression, self-confidence and a certain aloofness that does not lend itself to immediate and indiscriminate friendships. The dog must be approachable, quietly standing its ground and showing confidence and willingness to meet overtures without itself making them. It is poised, but when the occasion demands, eager and alert; both fit and willing to serve in its capacity as companion, watchdog, blind leader, herding dog, or guardian, whichever the circumstances may demand. The dog must not be timid, shrinking behind its master or handler; it should not be nervous, looking about or upward with anxious expression or showing nervous reactions, such as tucking of tail, to strange sounds or sights. Lack of confidence under any surroundings is not typical of good character. Any of the above deficiencies in character which indicate shyness must be penalized as very serious faults and any dog exhibiting pronounced indications of these must be excused from the ring. It must be possible for the judge to observe the teeth and to determine that both testicles are descended. Any dog that attempts to bite the judge must be disqualified. The ideal dog is a working animal with an incorruptible character combined with body and gait suitable for the arduous work that constitutes its primary purpose.

Head—The head is noble, cleanly chiseled, strong without coarseness, but above all not fine, and in proportion to the body. The head of the male is distinctly masculine, and that of the bitch distinctly feminine. The muzzle is long and strong with the lips firmly fitted, and its topline is parallel to the topline of the skull. Seen from the front, the forehead is only moderately arched, and the skull slopes into the long, wedge-shaped muzzle without abrupt stop. Jaws are strongly developed. *Ears*—Ears are moderately pointed, in proportion to the skull, open toward the front, and carried erect when at attention, the ideal carriage being one in which the center lines of the ears, viewed from the front, are parallel to each other and perpendicular to the ground. A dog with cropped or hanging ears must be disqualified. *Eyes*—Of medium size, almond shaped, set a little obliquely and not protruding. The color is as dark as possible. The expression keen, intelligent and composed. *Teeth*—42 in number—20 upper and 22 lower—are strongly developed and meet in a scissors bite in which part of the inner surface of the upper scissors meet and engage part of the outer surface of the lower incisors. An overshot jaw or a level bite is undesirable.

An undershot jaw is a disqualifying fault. Complete dentition is to be preferred. Any missing teeth other than first premolars is a serious fault.

Neck—The neck is strong and muscular, clean-cut and relatively long, proportionate in size to the head and without loose folds of skin. When the dog is at attention or excited, the head is raised and the neck carried high; otherwise typical carriage of the head is forward rather than up and but little higher than the top of the shoulders, particularly in motion.

Forequarters—The shoulder blades are long and obliquely angled, laid on flat and not placed forward. The upper arm joins the shoulder blade at about a right angle. Both the upper arm and the shoulder blade are well muscled. The forelegs, viewed from all sides, are straight and the bone oval rather than round. The pasterns are strong and springy and angulated at approximately a 25-degree angle from the vertical.

Feet—The feet are short, compact, with toes well arched, pads thick and firm, nails short and dark. The dewclaws, if any, should be removed from the hind legs. Dewclaws on the forelegs may be removed, but are normally left on.

Proportion—The German Shepherd Dog is longer than tall, with the most desirable proportion as 10 to 8½. The desired height for males at the top of the highest point of the shoulder blade is 24 to 26 inches; and for bitches, 22 to 24 inches. The length is measured from the point of the prosternum or breast bone to the rear edge of the pelvis, the ischial tuberosity.

Body—The whole structure of the body gives an impression of depth and solidity without bulkiness. *Chest*—Commencing at the prosternum, it is well filled and carried well down between the legs. It is deep and capacious, never shallow, with ample room for lungs and heart, carried well forward, with the prosternum showing ahead of the shoulder in profile. *Ribs*—Well sprung and long, neither barrel-shaped nor too flat, and carried down to a sternum which reaches to the elbows. Correct ribbing allows the elbows to move back freely when the dog is at a trot. Too round causes interference and throws the elbows out; too flat or short causes pinched elbows. Ribbing is carried well back so that the loin is relatively short. *Abdomen*—Firmly held and not paunchy. The bottom line is only moderately tucked up in the loin.

Topline—*Withers*—The withers are higher than and sloping into the level back. *Back*—The back is straight, very strongly developed without sag or roach, and relatively short. The desirable long proportion is not derived from a long back, but from over-all length with relation to height, which is achieved by length of forequarter and length of withers and hindquarter, viewed from the side. *Loin*—Viewed from the top, broad and strong. Undue length between the last rib and the thigh, when viewed from the side, is undesirable. *Croup*—Long and gradually sloping.

Tail—Bushy, with the last vertebra extended at least to the hock joint. It is set smoothly into the croup and low rather than high. At rest, the tail hangs in a slight curve like a saber. A slight look—sometimes carried to one side—is faulty only to the extent that it mars general appearance. When the dog is excited or in motion, the curve is accentuated and the tail raised, but it should never be curled forward beyond a vertical line. Tails too short, or with clumpy ends due to ankylosis, are serious faults. A dog with a docked tail must be disqualified.

Hindquarters—The whole assembly of the thigh, viewed from the side, is broad, with both upper and lower thigh well muscled, forming as nearly as possible a right angle. The upper thigh bone parallels the shoulder blade while the lower thigh bone parallels the upper arm. The metatarsus (the unit between the hock joint and the foot) is short, strong and tightly articulated.

Gait—A German Shepherd Dog is a trotting dog, and its structure has been developed to meet the requirements of its work. *General Impression*—The gait is outreaching, elastic, seemingly without effort, smooth and rhythmic, covering the maximum amount of ground with a minimum number of steps. At a walk it covers a great deal of ground, with long stride of both hind legs and forelegs. At a trot the dog covers still more ground with even longer stride, and moves powerfully but easily, with co-ordination and balance so that the gait appears to be the steady motion of a well-lubricated machine. The feet travel close to the ground on both forward reach and backward push. In order to achieve ideal movement of this kind, there must be good muscular development and ligamentation. The hindquarters deliver, through the back, a powerful forward thrust which slightly lifts the whole animal and drives the body forward. Reaching far under, and passing the imprint left by the front foot, the hind foot takes hold of the ground; then hock, stifle and upper thigh come into play and sweep back, the stroke of the hind leg finishing with the foot still close to the ground in a smooth follow-through. The over-reach of the hindquarter usually necessitates one hind foot passing outside and the other hind foot passing inside the track of the forefeet, and such action is not faulty unless the locomotion is crabwise with the dog's body sideways out of the normal straight line.

Transmission—The typical smooth, flowing gait is maintained with great strength and firmness of back. The whole effort of the hindquarter is transmitted to the forequarter through the loin, back and withers. At full trot, the back must remain firm and level without sway, roll, whip or roach. Unlevel topline with withers lower than the hip is a fault. To compensate for the forward motion imparted by the hindquarters, the shoulder should open to its full extent. The forelegs should reach out close to the ground in a long stride in harmony with that of the hindquarters. The dog does not track on widely separated parallel lines, but brings the feet inward toward the middle line of the body when trotting in order to maintain balance. The feet track closely but do not strike or cross over. Viewed from the front, the front legs function from the shoulder joint to the pad in a straight line. Viewed from the rear, the hind legs function from the hip joint to the pad in a straight line. Faults of gait, whether from front, rear or side, are to be considered very serious faults.

Color—The German Shepherd Dog varies in color, and most colors are permissible. Strong rich colors are preferred. Nose black.

Pale, washed-out colors and blues or livers are serious faults. A white dog or a dog with a nose that is not predominantly black, must be disqualified.

Coat—The ideal dog has a double coat of medium length. The outer coat should be as dense as possible, hair straight, harsh and lying close to the body. A slightly wavy outer coat, often of wiry texture, is permissible. The head, including the inner ear and foreface, and the legs and paws are covered with short hair, and the neck with longer and thicker hair. The rear of the forelegs and hind legs has somewhat longer hair extending to the pastern and hock, respectively. Faults in coat include soft, silky, too long outer coat, woolly, curly, and open coat.

DISQUALIFICATIONS

Cropped or hanging ears.

Undershot jaw.

Docked tail.

White dogs.

Dogs with noses not predominantly black.

Any dog that attempts to bite the judge.

Am. & Can. Ch. Covy-Tucker Hill's Finnegan, top winning U.S. Shepherd for 1976, 1977, 1978 and 1979. Winner Quaker Oats Award, 1977 (most group wins—all breeds). Finnegan's total wins: 195 Bests of Breed, 90 Working Group Firsts and 20 Bests in Show. By Covy's Oregano of Tucker-Hill, ROM ex Covy's Fate of Tucker-Hill, he was bred by Gloria Birch and Cappy Pottle, and is owned by Ralph S. and Mary Roberts.

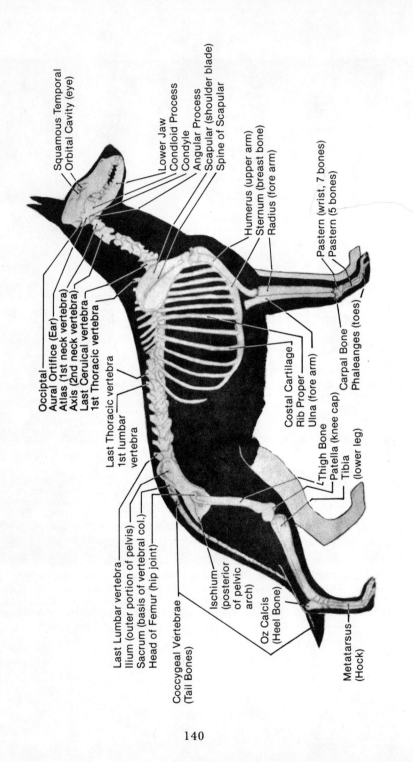

Squamous Temporal
Orbital Cavity (eye)

Lower Jaw
Condloid Process
Condyle
Angular Process
Scapular (shoulder blade)
Spine of Scapular

Humerus (upper arm)
Sternum (breast bone)
Radius (fore arm)

Pastern (wrist, 7 bones)
Pastern (5 bones)

Occiptal
Aural Ortifice (Ear)
Atlas (1st neck vertebra)
Axis (2nd neck vertebra)
Last Cervical vertebra
1st Thoracic vertebra

Last Thoracic vertebra
1st lumbar
vertebra

Costal Cartilage
Rib Proper
Ulna (fore arm)

Carpal Bone
Phaleanges (toes)

Last Lumbar vertebra
Ilium (outer portion of pelvis)
Sacrum (basis of vertebral col.)
Head of Femur (hip joint)

Ischium
(posterior
of pelvic
arch)

Thigh Bone
Patella (knee cap)
Tibia
(lower leg)

Coccygeal Vertebrae
(Tail Bones)

Oz Calcis
(Heel Bone)

Metatarsus
(Hock)

140

6

Blueprint of the German Shepherd Dog

THE affection of the owner for his German Shepherd Dog is seldom predicated upon its comparative excellence as a show dog. Character, temperament, responsiveness, intelligence, and the ability to perform the services for which he is trained and used is to the owner more important than the conformation to a physical ideal. How many of us would not prefer to possess another Rin Tin Tin, a dog without any of the qualifications of a great show dog, than to have the greatest champion that ever lived?

The difficulty of developing the personalities and temperaments of a large number of dogs at the same time makes the breeding of German Shepherd Dogs in wholesale numbers an insuperable task. Other breeds may be reared in the kennels, duly fed and cared for, and left to themselves. The mentality of the German Shepherd Dog is so highly organized that he stagnates or becomes neurotic without human companionship which he craves.

Much of the shyness and the sharpness and other undesirable temperaments observed in the breed are not inherited but are conditioned by neglect, indifference, ill treatment, or some avoidable or unavoidable mental trauma that the dog has suffered. Of course some German Shepherd Dogs are more alert and receptive to the regimen of training than others, but almost any young German Shepherd Dog can be developed into an agreeable and responsive companion and many of them can be taught to perform routine duties. A few can be developed into super dogs with what appears to be a strong faculty to reason like a human being.

However much the mental attributes of the German Shepherd Dog may overweigh his physical appearance, the ability to exercise his mental faculties depends at least in part on his physique. The joy of possessing an intelligent dog is doubly enhanced by having that intelligence encased in a beautiful, sound, and symmetrical body. Even if a leggy, square dog could function as well as one of correct proportions, the rightly-constructed animal is a joy to watch. The economy of effort in the well-made dog is a never ceasing source of satisfaction.

Why A Standard of Perfection?

It is to be admitted that correct construction in the German Shepherd Dog is a convention. But it is much more than a convention. It is not merely arbitrary. There is a reason behind every specification which the standard lays down.

The standard, however, merely establishes the specifications; it does not explain them. The standards of dog breeds are established by the specialty clubs (subject to the approval of the American Kennel Club) and are intended to describe dogs most fitted to perform the tasks for which the respective breeds are to be used. They are guides to perfection in the breed.

However, the most expertly written standard, while fully comprehensible to persons trained in the application of standards to living animals, may be mere jargon to the amateur or novice owner of a dog.

It is the function of the standard to describe the breed as briefly as possible. It describes an ideal. There is no room or place in it for an elucidation of the reasons behind that ideal, and, even in the statement of the ideal, it is not always as specific as it might be.

Moreover, standards do not describe faults in detail. *They are concerned with perfection, setting forth what a perfect dog shall be—not what he shall not be.* The economy of space precludes argument within the standard.

This is not to say however, that there is no room for argument outside the standard. Everybody who seeks to apply it has a slightly different concept about its meaning. Otherwise, judges would not vary as they do in making awards. Even when they do not differ about the meaning of the standard's terms, there is no absolute consensus about the comparative importance of the respective parts of the dog.

While the standard is designed to define and describe the perfect German Shepherd Dog, perfection does not exist. There is no perfect dog. Even among the greatest champions, perfection is merely approximated. A dog is not discredited and disqualified by a few or many minor deviations from the standard description. In judging the breed, the judge is not expecting a perfect dog; he must choose the best dogs in the classes that come before him. It is the judge's perogative to withhold ribbons if he considers specimens not worthy of ribbons.

However, in evaluating one's own stock for breeding, each individual *should* be judged against the standard.

It is not surprising then that judicial opinions should vary somewhat. What is more amazing is that judges should concur so much and so often as they do. While in the dog shows a dog may win on one day under one judge and be defeated the following day against the same competition under another judge, it is usually to be found the same group of dogs gravitate to the tops of the classes and a less excellent group are left out of the awards in both shows. The order in which the good dogs are placed may vary, but there is little difference in judicial opinion about what is excellent and what is mediocre.

It is sometimes possible to find out in advance of a show what idiosyncrasies or prejudices a judge may hold and to show a dog under a judge predisposed to like his style, or to withhold from the show a dog of the style that the judge does not like. For instance, although there is no valid preference between a gray dog and a black-and-tan, certain judges exercise a prejudice for or against certain colors. To exhibit a gray dog under a judge who habitually gives his prizes to a black-and-tan without regard to the fundamental merits of the exhibits is to court defeat.

Some judges simply refuse to give prizes to dogs with missing pre-molars (a minor fault) and will place a definitely inferior animal over another, no matter how good, with a gap in his mouth. Others may penalize a light eye to the same extent. It is hazardous to expose a dog to the tender mercies of a judge who is over-emphatic in his penalties for the particular fault the dog may possess.

Thus we see why there is nothing final about the position a dog may take in the award list of a single show. This is the reason for the rules which required a dog to win in a series of shows to obtain the title

The Maur-ray Kennels became established as the premier breeder of black German Shepherd Dogs in America. Pictured with owner Maureen Yentzen are four consecutive generations of homebred black bitches—Ch. Gerda of Maur-ray, finished in 1951; Gerda's daughter, Ch. Marlene of Maur-ray, finished in 1953; and Marlene's daughter, Ch. Wilma of Maur-ray, finished in 1955. At left is Wilma's daughter, Ch. Arla of Maur-ray, finished in 1959.

of champion. Otherwise, one show would settle everything. The position of a dog in the prize list of a single show is no final criterion of his merits or the lack of them.

Judges are reluctant, if they are not too tired after a day's work, to give an owner of a dog an opinion about it more than is contained in the dog's position in the awards. They wish not to add the insult of criticism of the dog to the injury of having placed it low in the prize list. They seek to avoid argument and above all wish not to be misquoted, which they frequently are.

One extremely astute all-breed judge had a humorous answer for the often heard "The judge last week gave me the blue, why didn't you?" "I can't be held responsible for someone else's mistakes," was this judge's method of avoiding discussion. Another often retorted with "Sir, he must have liked your dog more than I did."

Many judges, usually those who are doing one breed only can, and will, take the time to tell an exhibitor what he finds good or not so good about an animal. However, no judge should be asked to do this until all his assignment has been completed. Nor should judges be expected to defend their placings. However, all-breed judges, many of whom are judging entries of 170 dogs that day, do not have time to give more than a cursory opinion of an exhibit outside the ring and feel that your dog has been rated by them inside the ring, thus any more discussion is redundant.

It therefore behooves the owner to evaluate his own dog, unless he wishes to take the dog to a series of shows to ascertain the truth about it. Most owners do not want to take their dog even to one show to have the dog disparaged or ridiculed. An owner may not necessarily expect to win, but he wants to know before he exhibits the dog that it is worthy of being exhibited. He can make his own survey. While he may not be able to determine from such a survey whether or not the dog can achieve a championship, being unaware of the competition the dog may encounter, he can determine whether it is or is not worthy to be exhibited at all.

In the early twenties, following upon the movie success of Strongheart and Rin Tin Tin, the country went "police dog" mad. Mediocre and even positively bad dogs were bred from to supply a market that would absorb at high prices any puppy that had four legs, prick ears, and a tail. The German breeders exported to America at high prices all the near-mongrels they could lay their hands upon. There was a German Shepherd Dog craze, like the tulip craze in Holland or the Belgian Hare craze of the early part of the century. Anything that could pretend to be a German Shepherd Dog was treasured, valued, and like as not exhibited. Long, short, high, low, sound or crippled, anything that even resembled a German Shepherd Dog was accepted as a "police dog."

The craze was so great that the reaction to it was equally violent. From such an influx of mediocrity the good dogs of the breed were bound to suffer. It had been a mark of distinction to own a German Shepherd Dog. The breed has large litters and it multiplied itself rapidly. Prices fell. The bottom had dropped out. The breed was out of favor and out of fashion. It was not to be wondered at that such enthusiasm could not last.

However, a group of persistent and discriminating fanciers stuck to the breed through thick and thin. While the Germans were shipping to America all the trash they could produce, astute American buyers were acquiring the very best and greatest of the

A long campaign in England to give the breed the German Shepherd Dog identification it carries elsewhere throughout the world won out in 1979. Until then, the breed was called the Alsatian. One of the high spots in its history there was the win of Best in Show at Crufts' 1969 (over an entry of 7,786 dogs all breeds) by Eng. Ch. Hendrawen's Nibelung of Charavigne, lovely bitch owned by Mr. and Mrs. E.J. White, and handled by Mr. White.

Ch. Caralon's Phantom of Leberland, an outstanding black son of ROM sire Ch. Caralon's Hein von der Lockehein, CD. Owned by Timothy H. Hille.

German output, which the German monetary inflation enabled them to do, breeding steadily and carefully from these truly great dogs. They were more lenient in regard to soundness and trueness in purging it of its inferior blood and in developing strains that bred true for desirable attributes. The results were better individual dogs and a breed of higher average excellence than ever before in the breed's history. This resulted in an increase in public interest in the breed, not as a craze or fad but as a serious and persistent interest.

Judging Your Dog

Accordingly, it is necessary in looking at a dog to seek for a high state of excellence. Mediocrity will not suffice. To be good at all, a present day dog must be very good.

Let us take your dog out on the lawn or in the park and have a look at him. The German Shepherd Dog requires space. He does not look his best in cramped or constricted quarters. The rings alloted to the judging of German Shepherd Dogs in many all-breed dog shows are not spacious enough to enable the judges to see the exhibits to best advantage. What is needed is an open space at least a hundred feet long, and more can be utilized. Type can be examined in comparatively small space, but even for that purpose it is necessary to stand away from the dog in order to see him whole, as well as to stand close enough to handle him and examine the individual parts. But gait is the test of structure, a statement that we shall have occasion to repeat, and space is required to examine the dog's action.

Indeed, the gait of a German Shepherd Dog is as important as the gait of a horse, and the largest part of our survey leads up to our examination of the dog for action. The gait can be largely predicated from the dog's make and shape, but it must be confirmed.

When, in the 1920s and '30s, German authorities came to America to judge and to vent their fads and fancies, which they did to accord with the dogs they or other German fanciers had to sell, they were very emphatic in their insistence upon a powerful drive in their winning dogs. They were more lenient in regard to soundness and trueness of movement than were American judges. A dog might be cowhocked or out at the elbow, he might be scrawny, insignificant, or yellow eyed, but to satisfy these Germans he had to cover a short distance with asserted vigor and reserve of power. (Few German judges have judged at shows in America in recent years, but those who have seem to prefer much the same dogs as our better judges.)

We shall return to consideration of gait after we have considered the structure of the dog and the application of the standard.

Type

The word "type" is erroneously used by many dog-show ringsiders and would-be authorities. The word has been misused so often that it has left many novices confused, and they in turn pass on the misinformation.

Are *you* confused? You need not be. Just keep in mind that a typy German Shepherd Dog is one that displays conformation, sex

A handsome exemplar of German Shepherd Dog type, Canadian Grand Victor Am. Ch. Danka's El Malachi.

Another fine model of breed type, Ch. Peddacres Uno, CD, owned by Roger and Ann Gafke.

Ch. Tucker Hill's Oracle, UDT, our cover dog, pictured at 8½ years. Owned by Louise M. and William G. Penery.

characteristics, expression and temperament considered desirable and representative of the breed.

There cannot be more than one type within our breed. There can be only variations of the type required, and we should all avoid them, and strive to breed as closely to the ideal standard type as possible. All breeders should aim to approximate the desirable type, and all judges must (or should) prefer only the standard type. The choice in the ring should attempt to bring to the fore those animals that vary least from the ideal.

Of course the condition of the animal has much to do with determining its merits. In any event the dog should be clean, thoroughly well-fed on a balanced diet, free from intestinal parasites, clear-eyed, with teeth free from slime, dirt or tartar, and with skin free from lesions, whether produced by injury or disease. He should have been brought with judicious exercise to a high state of physical vigor and firmness of muscle. His nails should be shortened enough to give compactness to the feet, but not to injure the quick.

The state of the coat is not material for the purposes of this examination, since it is a temporary matter and subject to shedding in any event. Allowance can be made for the dog's ability to grow a coat, and even the tearing out of the undercoat, whether by accident or design, does not affect the animal's fundamental excellence. Of course the absence of undercoat may possibly affect the position of the dog in the official prize list of a dog show, but in such an unofficial survey as we are making. his known ability to grow a coat is more important than his actual possession of an underjacket.

The expert handling of the dog may also be discounted. Anybody who can lead and pose the dog for us will suffice. It is the function of the professional dog handler to present the dog to the judge in the most favorable light, to emphasize its favorable attributes and to conceal its faults. The German Shepherd Dog is so forthright an animal that even the cleverest handler is unable to deceive a good judge. There is nothing to trim, nothing to conceal, nothing to fake. Moreover, in this survey we wish to arrive at a true evaluation of the dog for *our own* satisfaction. We are not seeking to have ourselves deceived. An amateur handler is for our purposes even better than the expert, somebody who will follow our instructions about the dog's pose and about moving him.

The slip chain collar is conventional for the breed, and does not so interrupt the sweep of the eye over the whole dog as does a leather collar. The lead should be of leather, more than a yard in length, strong enough to control the dog in any emergency but light enough not to be cumbersome.

Size

The size of the German Shepherd Dog is, within limits, not of great importance. The standard defines the ideal height, established by taking a perpendicular line from the top of the shoulder blade to the ground with the coat parted or so pushed down that the measurement will show only the actual height of the frame or structure of the dog, as 24 to 26 inches for dogs, and between 22 and 24 inches for bitches. A dog of standard size is sometimes criticized by the uninformed, and to some degree by the informed, as being too small.

Clumsiness and an excess of bone are faults, whether they be found in dogs of regulation height or in dogs with an excess of height

151

as set down in the standard. They are faults in themselves, without reference to the size of the dog that manifests them.

The Head

The description of the head given us in the standard is adequate for the purposes. The structure of the head is within limits a comparatively minor consideration in judging the German Shepherd Dog.

There is no scale of points in the standard, and it must remain an idiosyncrasy of the individual judge as to just what allotment he is to make for head structure in his analysis of the entire dog. Von Stephanitz in his unofficial scale of points allots five points in his scale of 100 to head, in which he includes mouth, eyes, and ears. This is preposterously insufficient, since with such calculation it would be possible for a dog with a good body and gait to win despite a clublike head, yellow eye, overshot mouth, and lopped ears. On the other hand, some exquisite heads, perfect mouths, dark eyes, and superb ears are attached to and followed by intolerable bodies and running gear. For the dog to pass inspection at all the head must be characteristic, although a dog may be a good one with a head structure that is far from perfect. We can only say that body, legs and feet are of considerably greater importance than mere beauty of head.

The head of the German Shepherd Dog is not a finely drawn one, but it has the "quality" that marks nobility. Let us dispose at once of the tradition that the width of a dog's head has anything at all to do with its intelligence, else the Bulldog would be the most intelligent of dogs and the Terrier the most stupid. The brainpan of the dog is comparatively small, and the animal's intelligence has nothing whatever to do with the size of the brain, but rather with the amount or number of its convolutions. There is no need to fear that in the refinement of head of the German Shepherd Dog we are courting stupidity.

The muzzle should be well carried out. If it has the depth and power required, there is little reason to fear that it can be too long. This statement is made despite the caution of Von Stephanitz and other German authorities. This muzzle is wedge-shaped. The stop is small, a mere demarcation between the top-skull and the top line of the muzzle, which should be parallel to the top surface of the skull, neither down-faced nor dish-faced.

152

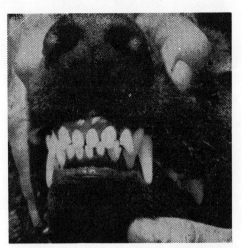

A scissors bite.

Teeth

The formation of the teeth becomes important: first, because the teeth are employed in the dog's work and, secondly, because the structure of the mouth and teeth is heritable. The scissors bite is described in the standard, with the inner surface of the upper incisors meeting and engaging the outer surface of the lower incisors. There is a valid reason for this type of bite. The erosion of the incisors with the pincer bite (one in which the edges of the teeth meet directly) is much greater than with the scissors formation. A three-or four-year-old dog with a pincer bite will display incisors worn well nigh to the gum, while a sound scissors mouth may last as long as the dog.

The undershot mouth (one in which the lower teeth protrude beyond the upper teeth) is seldom to be found in the German Shepherd Dog. When it is observed, the animal is to be disqualified. Its opposite number, the overshot mouth is much more prevalent. While the over-elongation of the jaw is not to be feared for its own sake, the overshot jaw which accompanies it must be penalized, for, with the tight, "dry" lips of the breed, it gives the face a chinless-wonder aspect, makes of the dog a canine Andy Gump.

Some judges make a fetish of counting the four pre-molars to be found on each side of each jaw, and to such judges one such missing tooth condemns the whole dog. The German judges in one era introduced the counting of these teeth as a fad and some of their American sycophants adhered to it. However, having any teeth missing other than first pre-molars is a serious fault.

153

Ears

There is little to add to the description of the ears as given in the standard, except that in "discarding" cropped or hanging ears we also discard the whole dog that carries them.

Nothing adds to the nobility and animation of a German Shepherd Dog more than well-placed and carried ears. He talks with them. Weak or lopped ears are a perennial problem in the breed. Erect-eared parents frequently produce progeny with soft ears, although one parent with soft ears mated to another with correct ears may produce puppies with erect ears. The statement in the standard that dogs with cropped or hanging ears must be disqualified helps to eliminate from breeding stock the hereditary fault of soft ears.

Small, pointed, stingy ears are more certain of erection than larger ones, but they are harmful to the expression. The ideal ear is generous in size without being disproportionately large, although it would be a captious critic who would penalize a dog for excessive ear size, provided that the ears were erect and active. Puppies with large ears, however, as a rule do not raise their ears as early as those with smaller ears, and just possibly will never raise them at all. An absolutely upright ear set directly on the top of the head makes the skull appear narrow and gives the dog a slightly "foreign" expression. Such ears are likely not to spread correctly and to "nick inward," if not to fall toward the center of the head, due to a weakness of the erectile muscles.

Eyes

The description of the eyes in the German Shepherd Dog standard is unfortunate in not being more definitive. The best eyes are somewhat more than medium in size, only slightly ovoid or almond shaped. The expression should indeed be lively, composed, and intelligent. Dignity and a possible aloofness is acceptable, but any show of animosity is contra indicated. The most desirable eye is wide-spaced and generous. Narrowly spaced eyes give the animal stingy and querulous outlook, which is not characteristic of the breed.

While yellow eyes do not affect a dog's working ability, they spoil the appearance of an exhibition dog. Short of dead blackness and the absence of color differentiation between pupil and iris, the eye can hardly be too dark, and even that dead blackness is to be preferred to any of the shades of lemon.

The German Shepherd Dog is the most normally made and the least freakish of all the breeds of dogs and has fewer merely arbitrary qualifications that have nothing at all to do with its functions and purpose. The German Shepherd Dog is a unit and no part of it is to be overweighed or be considered separately from any other part. The structure of the parts behind the head determines the structure of the head. It will be found that a lean scrawny, narrow chested dog without substance is prone to carry an overly fine and elongated head, and a clumsy, cloddy dog with too much bone for its size is prone to carry a coarse, chunky, short head. Neither sort of dog is desirable. We want the maximum of agility plus an adequacy of power, which is obtainable without compromise.

We may now leave the head and consider the structure behind it.

Proportion

One of the most important factors concerning the German Shepherd Dog is the proportion of his length over all (not his length of back) to his height at the withers. His trotting gait depends upon this. The tall dog or one approaching squareness is intolerable.

It is all but impossible to make accurate measurements, but the approximate ratio called for in the standard is 10 to 8½. These measurements must be made by the eye, from the very front of the pro-sternum to the back of the buttocks and from the top of the shoulder blade to the ground. Allowance must be made for the length of the hair, which should not be included. That the dog shall be longer than high is of the utmost importance.

It is possible for a German Shepherd Dog to be so short of leg as to present a Dachshund-like appearance, but it is quite unlikely that the length in proportion to the height will be found too great. A dog with great depth of brisket appears lower on the leg than one that is too shallow, but unless the dog immediately appears deformed, short legs and long body remain a virtue.

The Neck

The German Shepherd Dog's neck reaches from its body to its head, a considerable distance—more than it appears in its ruff of hair. A dog with an upright shoulder will certainly have an inadequate length of neck. The base of the neck extends in a diagonal line along the shoulder blade from the forechest to the withers, and should be deep and thick as well as long. The depth of the neck as well as the thickness of the hair makes the neck appear shorter than it really is. It is in proportion to the head it is called upon to manipulate.

A slightly crested neck is an evidence of power, whereas an ewe-neck is a sign of weakness.

The neck should be free from dewlap or throatiness, a fault seldom found in the German Shepherd Dog. The German Shepherd Dog is a confident, high-headed dog. He has the carriage of head to be expected in any noble dog. In a fast trot he lowers his head for the sake of balance. Dogs with inadequate length or strength of neck are prone to slump, as is one with too coarse or heavy a head. But the normal head carriage is high and alert.

The Body

It is the body of the dog, rather than its back, that should be long. The back is comparatively short. The dog is not a pack animal and does not have to support weight upon its back, which nevertheless must be very firm for the transmission of energy from the hindquarters to the forehand, as will be discussed later.

Distinction must be made between the length of the body and the length of the back. The body extends from the point of the shoulders to the rear of the buttocks, whereas the back extends only from the withers to the pelvic bones. The back is the bridge to carry the power developed in the powerful hindquarters to the square shoulder formation. The forequarters develop no power of their own and merely serve as points of suspension to prevent the dog from falling forward on his face. Such being the case, the emphasis upon the correct shoulder and forehand may seem to be misplaced. However, a dog's step can be no longer than is permitted by the angle of the scapula or shoulder blade and the humerus or bone of the upper arm. This must be great enough to permit the front end of the dog to keep up with the hindquarters, which in the best dogs is approximately a right angle.

There is little point in having a powerful and well-angulated hindquarters to propel the animal without forequarters with a sufficient angle of shoulder to absorb the stride.

STRUCTURAL FAULTS

*Note: Dotted lines indicate faults in structure;
solid lines indicate the correct profile.*

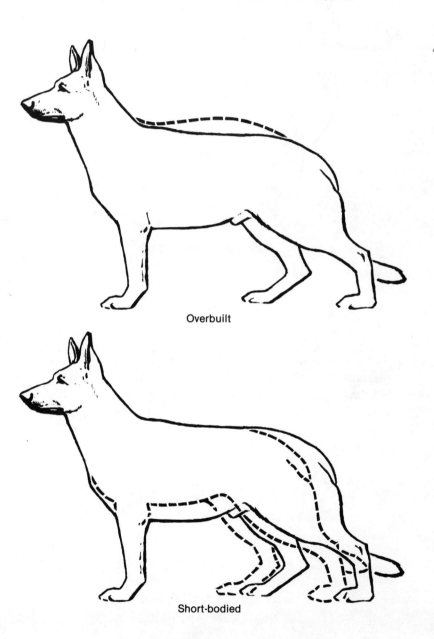

Overbuilt

Short-bodied

Swaying or hollow back.

High-legged, short-bodied, with drawn-up abdomen
and lacking depth of chest.

Carp back.

Sloping croup.

159

The back should be absolutely straight, level, and unroached from the pelvic bone to the shoulder blade. The idea, although so far as known it has never been practically attained, is a back upon which a glass brimful of water could rest without spilling with the dog at a straightaway trot. It is not implied that such a test shall be made; it is liable to be disappointing.

Any tendency of the back to sag or sway results in a loss of transmitted power and must be heavily penalized. A carp back or roached back, while not so reprehensible as an equal degree of sag, which is its opposite fault, denotes a constriction in the muscles of the loin which, to the extent of the roach, tends to destroy the dog's liberty. It results in a shortness of stride in the hindquarters and a greater expenditure of energy in covering ground.

While the dog overall should be long, and the back should be comparatively short, this does not mean as short as possible. While a short back is more efficient for a dog moving in a direct line, it does not admit of sinuosity, flexibility, and lithesomeness in quick turning, weaving, rising and stooping, for which the work of the German Shepherd Dog calls.

In depth of body, the chest should extend at least to the elbow of a fully matured dog. It may well be even deeper than that. No allowance is to be made for coat in such measurement. The German Shepherd Dog does not reach full maturity until it is two years, sometimes two and a half years old, and no final judgment of the depth of body can be reached before that approximate age.

The chest should be capacious with ample room for heart and lungs. This must be achieved by a wide spring of rib at the junction of rib and with the spine, followed by an abrupt drop of the rib. This leaves the sides of the dog flat. Such a formation offers a maximum of capacity with the least impediment to action. Barrel-like ribs, while they may be spectacular, do not provide the capacity they seem to hold; they cause the dog to wobble from side to side in his action and interfere with the play of his elbows.

Thoracic capacity is also achieved by the extension of the ribs horizontally. The chest should be long as possible as well as deep. This means, not that the German Shepherd Dog has more ribs than other dogs, but that the individual ribs are wider and wider spaced along the spine.

The loin is heavy and of moderate length. It must be long

enough for flexibility and short enough for strength. This is achieved by depth of loin. There is a minimum of tuck up of belly, although there is no paunch-like flabbiness. The great girth of loin is the result of solid, hard muscle. It is impossible to disguise too great a tuck up with fat pulling the belly down. That becomes a double fault. It is better to accept somewhat too much tuck up than to fill it in with soft flabbiness.

The croup of the German Shepherd Dog is exceedingly long, but not steep. It forms a gradual slope from the pelvis bones to the set-on of tail. It will be found in dogs with a level croup that their tendency is to carry their tails in the air — a terrier-like formation. Dogs with too abrupt a croup are hampered in their stride, appear short of body, and lack balance.

The croup leads into the tail, which is a mere continuation of the spine. The ideal length is that the tail itself, not merely the hair on it, shall reach to the point of the hock. Additional length, however, is not to be penalized. Greater difficulty is found in tails too short than in those too long; if noticeably too short, symmetry and balance of the entire animal are affected. Tails with clumpy ends due to ankylosis (abnormal immobility and consolidation of a joint) are serious faults. A dog with a docked tail must be disqualified.

When the dog is in repose, the tail should hang almost straight down, but with a slight saber curve to prevent an appearance of deadness. Twists or curls or kinks in the tail are, to put it mildly, undesirable.

In extreme animation or excitement a dog is likely to raise his tail, which is all right, but the tail should never rise so high as the vertical, much less turn over the dog's back. There is little likelihood of this occurring in a dog with a correctly formed croup.

The tail serves the dog as a rudder and is a practical part of its anatomy and affects the gait. Short tails are inadequate for the purpose, and a tail with a kink services the dog only down to the point where the kink begins. Beyond that point the tail is dead weight and a hindrance to the steering.

The German Shepherd Dog tail is never whiplike or fragile, and it is not sharply pointed. It forms a good handful and is a powerful instrument in the balancing and guiding of the dog in the making of quick turns.

Ch. Linnloch Brigadier, bred and owned by Dorothy Linn. A California winner.

<pre>
                                    GV Ch Troll v Richterbach ROM
                        Ch. Fortune of Arbywood ROM
                                    Frigga of Silver Lane ROM
            Ch Bach v Richaus
                                    Ch Fels of Arbywood ROM
            Ch Alexis v Richaus
                                    Sarego's Ansel
CH. LINNLOCH BRIGADIER
                                    Ch Fels of Arbywood ROM
                        Ch Gallant of Arbywood ROM
                                    Ch Arbywood's Dise
            Tucker Hill's Quesa CD
                                    Am & Can Ch Rosetown Bravado
                        Christy of Tucker Hill
                                    Tucker Hill's Renee of Miramar UD
</pre>

The Front

The German Shepherd Dog is an animal of extreme angulations both of the forehand and of the hindquarters, and it is largely by its angulation that the merits of a dog are evaluated. The angulation of the shoulder (that is the junction of the upper arm with the shoulder blade), as we have said, should be as nearly a right angle as possible, with the dog standing firmly and normally on the floor. Such an angle permits him the maximum opening of the forehand and the longest possible step. With a shoulder of such angulation is to be found a magnificent forechest with great depth of neck. There is no padding or bunchiness of shoulder muscles to be found with such a formation. The shoulder blade is extremely long, and of approximately equal length with the upper arm. The longer the better, and, with adequate angulation, the greater the forechest. It is this forechest that, in part, increases the length of the entire dog over its height.

From the upper arm the forearm drops straight to the pastern joint, turning neither in nor out. If it turns inward to make the dog appear pigeon-toed, it will be found that the dog is "out at elbow," the attachment of the shoulder blades to the body is not firm, and the dog will wobble in its action. Turning of the feet outward results from either of two faulty formations. The fault may be in too tight a shoulder, forcing the elbow close to the body, and the whole leg may be twisted outward, which usually is associated with a narrow, pigeon-breasted chest. Or the outward turn of the feet may result from a twist of the pastern joint, an effort of the organism to compensate for too narrow a chest and a consequently insecure stance. This latter formation is called "Frenching," from its resemblance to the position attributed to French dancing masters.

The pastern is moderately long and almost straight. There is in it a 25° give which saves the leg, as seen from the side, from being absolutely straight. This give in the pastern joint absorbs some of the shock in a rapid or prolonged trot. Too much of it, especially if accompanied with insufficient bone formation, is a source of weakness and lack of endurance. The absolutely straight, terrier-like front gives a stilty and awkward appearance to a dog, but in a choice between it and a broken down pastern, the straight front is to be chosen. A knuckled-over pastern and semblance of double joints is strongly reprehensible and subject to severe penalty.

The straight front is usually found with cat-like feet, the weak pastern with hare-like feet. Correct German Shepherd Dog feet

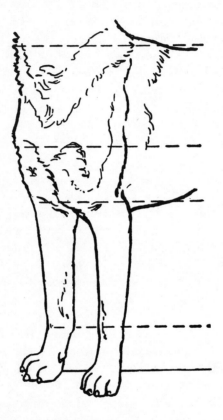

1. Good formation of chest and forelegs.

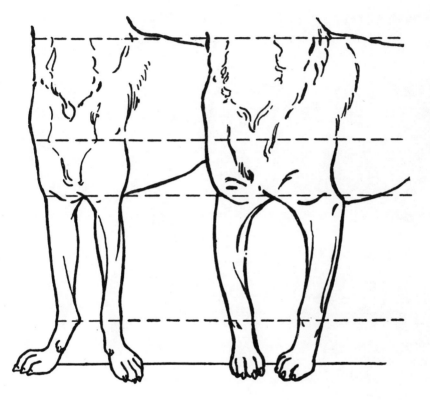

2. Faulty. Small chest, without depth, faulty prosternum, drawn out or loosely-knit body, drawn-in elbows, weak pasterns, stand like that of a dancing master.

3. Faulty. Broad, barrel-shaped chest, distended or turned-out elbows, bent lower arm, knees too wide apart giving a bad stand on the ground and the toes.

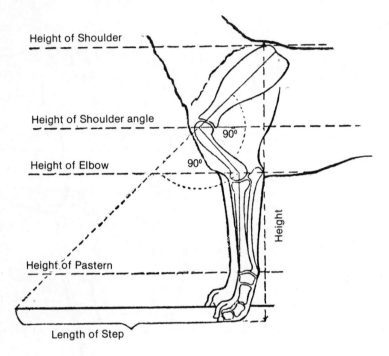

Height of Shoulder

Height of Shoulder angle

90°

Height of Elbow

90°

Height

Height of Pastern

Length of Step

1. Good formation of prosternum and lower sternum. Neck powerfully set, high long withers, strong bones and good leverage for the forelegs. Plenty of play for the shoulder, which makes a good long pace and advance possible.

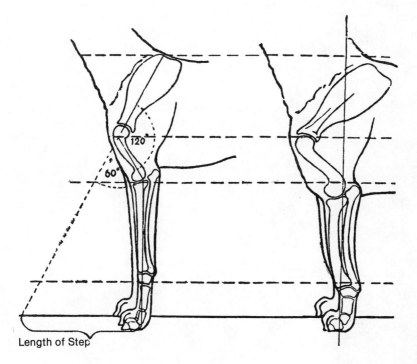

Length of Step

2. Faulty prosternum. Depth of chest too narrow, thin neck, low withers, bones too long and too thin. Faulty angles and accordingly faulty leverage for the limbs. Little play for the shoulder and consequently a short pace and advance. Pasterns long and too steep. Stork-like build with poor gait; deceptively appears to be good because of the long bones.

3. Faulty. Compressed formation of chest and neck, large bones shoulders somewhat advanced. Bent radius and ulna with distended joints (the result of weakness in the bones). Pasterns oversteep and short. Build is of a thick-set dog with bound rolling gait.

An impressive winner of the 1970s, Ch. Asslan von Klamme, SchH III, 1975-76 Select. Pictured in Group win under J.D. Jones. Owner, Miss Alexandra A. Peters. Handled by Lamar Kuhns.

neither cat-like nor hare-like, but midway between them in their length. A cat foot serves well enough for a dog traveling straight forward, but it was likely to burn in making a quick turn. What is more important than the mere length of the foot is its well knuckled compactness and depth of pad. Nails should be heavy and thick. Long thin nails are usually found on a thin, weak foot. Nails can, of course, be shortened, but a dog with good feet will with plenty of exercise keep his nails worn down sufficiently that they require little cutting back.

Looked at from the front, the legs are entirely straight and parallel one to the other. The front is neither wide nor narrow. A wide front impairs the dog's speed and agility, whereas a narrow front does not provide a stance to support the dog with the greatest ease.

The bone of the German Shepherd Dog is ample, without being massive. A dog with frail, fragile, inadequate bone will be unable to stand the gaff of persistent, hard work. On the other hand, too much bone, or soft and spongy bone, makes for lumbering clumsiness. Where choice must be made between too much bone and too little, too much is to be preferred. A dog is seldom criticized for his possession of a superfluity of bone. The formation of the bone of the lower arm is the usual criterion of the bone structure of the whole dog; if it is adequate, that of the rest of the dog may be depended upon to suffice.

The Rear

The hindquarters are formed with long bones, the thigh bone being at an approximate right angle with the hip bone, with the dog standing normally, and the stifle bones at right angle to the thigh bone. The hock drops vertically from the hock joint. Such a formation gives the dog the maximum of leverage and propulsive power. This is of extreme importance.

The dog should be permitted to stand normally during its examination. The efforts on the part of some exhibitors to stretch the hindquarters and to place the feet, or one of them, as far back as is possible deceives nobody except the veriest novice. In the show ring it is not unusual to see dogs stretched all out of shape until the rear of the dog looks like a pair of props and the front legs are thrown off the perpendicular in the dog's effort to compensate for the extreme stretching of the hindquarters and to keep his balance. A correctly-made dog

169

HINDLEGS, EARS AND TAIL
(Dog Standing Still)

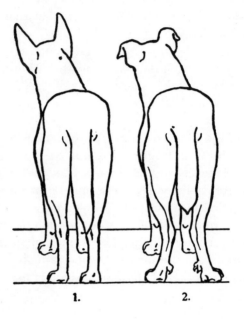

1. 2.

1. Good stand and position.

2. Faulty. Knock-kneed, legs like riding britches. Dewclaws (single on left foot, double on right foot). Double spurs. Ears badly tipping over (too heavy). Stumpy tail.

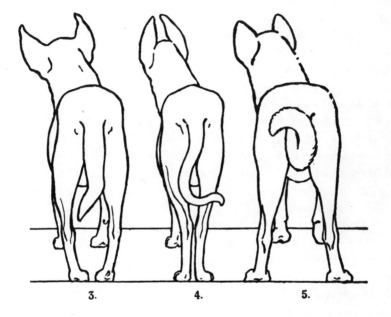

3. Faulty. Bandy-legged. Ears too large and too deep-set. Slightly hook-like tail, bending sideways.

4. Faulty. Weak, sidewards-sloping buttocks, like a pig. Turned-out knees. Fox-like loins. Bad position on the ground. Ears too near together, too thin and too long. Tail bent sideways.

5. Faulty. Broad, coarse buttocks with broad steep stand. Bear's feet. Short thick ears. Beginning of a ring tail.

can be posed with the lead to exhibit his extreme angulation; it does not require the stretching out of the dog by hand with the admonition to him to hold his pose. Many judges rightly resent this artificial posing of the dog, and, in the effort to examine the dog in his normal position, ask that the handler break the pose by moving the dog by a step or two. Some handlers are so persistent in their efforts to distort the natural position that they immediately set about stretching their dog artificially again and the judge is compelled to break the pose again and again. Some handlers will persist in this artificial stretching of their dogs in the face of specific instructions from the judge that the dogs shall be permitted to pose themselves naturally.

The exact angles of the various bones are impossible to state since they depend upon the position assumed by the hindquarters. The estimated ideal of 90 degrees each at pelvis and stifle joints is for an ideal dog with a normal stance with a vertical line from the ischium tuberosity to the horizontal floor passing through the foot immediately in front of the hock. By stretching the dog's quarters, while it gives an optical illusion of greater length, the angulation is made less acute rather than more acute.

This bony structure should be as large and substantial as possible and the bones should be extremely long. To manipulate these vast levers the muscles must be long and powerful and their attachments must be strong. The hams are immense, both in depth and thickness.

Such a formation enables the animal to take a long, flexible stride, the power of which is transferred to the spine and carried by it to the forequarters. The shoulder joint must be acute enough to open wide to accommodate the length of step of the hindquarters, else the power is lost and the step is shortened.

There should be no interference of one hock with the other, but the rear stance of the breed is comparatively narrow. The legs must never appear to spraddle. The hocks should be absolutely parallel one to the other, standing or moving. Any tendency toward barrel or bandy legs on the one hand or toward cow-hocks on the other hand is a sign of unsoundness and is not to be tolerated.

Cow-hocks sometimes result from excessive high jumping especially in puppyhood, in which case they tend not to reappear in the dog's progeny. However, the larger part of cow-hocks are inherited and tend to be transmitted to the progeny. It is unsafe to breed from a cow-hocked dog. Judges have no way of knowing whether cow-hocks are acquired or inherited, and therefore have no alternative but to penalize them whenever they are found. Cow-hocks are a serious fault.

Learning to stand for evaluation early.

In the craze for excessive angulation of the hindquarters there has developed a tendency for the hocks to turn forward from the vertical when the dog is standing at ease. This formation is often referred to as "saber hocks." Its effect is the weakening of the hock joint, an added tension upon the muscles. Saber hocks are deceptive in that at first consideration they appear as added angulation, but the angulation is in the wrong place. They are spectacular and may fool the uninitiated, but they exemplify weakness rather than strength.

Coat

The coat of the German Shepherd Dog may be of various lengths, textures, natures, and qualities. However, in America only the smooth coat is found and accepted. This smooth coat is found with some variation in length and density, but it is essentially alike on all dogs, and it is seldom open to much criticism.

It consists in a pily, woolly, slightly oily underjacket through which grow long, straight guard hairs. The head is comparatively smooth, the front legs smooth with a fringe of slightly longer hair at the back, a heavy coat around the neck and on the back, and a profuse growth of hair on the hips and tail. There is some variation in the profusion of coat in summer and winter weather.

The coat of a German Shepherd Dog, except for its condition, is seldom open to criticism. The guard hairs on the back will range in length from 1½ inches to 2½ inches, although without measuring the coat it may not appear to be so long. The shorter hair gives a dog a deceptive refinement of outline, which is not truly characteristic of the breed. The longer hair is, on the whole, to be preferred. While the absolutely correct coat is straight, a slightly crinkled or curled coat is not highly objectionable. Such crinkled coats are likely to be of heavier texture and less dense than one with straight guard hairs.

While little is likely to be found wrong with the nature of the coat, its condition is so important that it may defeat a dog entered in competition. That is must be healthy, alive, and lustrous goes without saying. Excessive grooming with a fine comb or rake may pull out the undercoat, leaving the guard hair lying flat to the skin, or the dog may simply fail to grow an undercoat. When it has been pulled out through excessive grooming it will grow again and no harm may accrue. A judge has no means of knowing whether a dog lacking undercoat fails to grow one or whether it has been pulled out. That undercoat is essential to a dog as protection against excessive heat, cold, sleet, rain, or snow, and even against insect bites. The German Shepherd Dog is an all-weather dog, and, while in America he seldom is compelled to rough it, he must have a protective covering that enables him to endure unfavorable conditions. Along with his superior intelligence, it is accommodation to all climates and environments that makes him the best all around dog for any purpose—in addition to his specific function as a herdsman.

Rich colors are preferred in the coat. Dogs with faded pigment are undesirable and white dogs are disqualified in the show ring.

Dewclaws

Dewclaws are fifth toes sometimes found on the inside of the hock and on forefeet. They are unslightly and are usually removed surgically while the puppy is in the nest. They tend to appear as recessives in certain strains and are to be avoided. Just why they should interfere with the action of the dog that carries them is not clear, but the fact is that a dog with dewclaws seldom moves well. The dewclaw may be on only one hock or both. Less frequently they are found in double form with two extra toes, with two nails, on each foot.

Ch. Ricella's Frigga, one of the all-time top winning bitches, with 2 all-breed Bests in Show, 7 Specialty Bests in Show and 45 Bests of Breed to her credit. Select at the 1965 and 1966 Specialties. Bred and owned by Dr. C.R. Peluso and handled by Denise Kodner.

Am. & Can. Ch. Fant Wikingerblut, SchH III, Canadian Grand Victor for 1963. A Best in Show winning son of Ulk. Owned by Marion Darling.

A grand picture of German Shepherd Dog absorption. Ch. Cita v. Da-Rie-Mar-Hill, CD, Ch. Calipho of Villa Marina, and Cita's puppies. Owned by Mr. and Mrs. Raymond C. Becker.

A Picture of Your Dog

We have now gone carefully over the dog and examined him critically. We have explored him with the hands as well as with the eyes. We have found major or minor faults in his structure and have noted those departments and attributes in which he particularly excels. We have perhaps been able to stand our dog alongside another of acknowledged excellence and noted the differences between them. We have at least been able to compare the dog with the pictures of great dogs shown in this book.

It is to be remembered that no dog is perfect, and in any comparison with a living dog or with a pictured one allowance must be made for the possibility that in some details the dog under examination may excel the other. Dogs are photographed in positions to exploit their best features and to conceal their shortcomings. Photographs are even sometimes faked and doctored to make dogs appear better than they are. This must be taken into consideration before we condemn a dog for some minor fault wherein he appears to fall short, or praise him on the strength of some particularly striking picture.

In many pictures, the subject is stretched and drawn out in a mistaken effort to make the dog appear long and to accent his angulation. Just because your dog when posed naturally is not stretched all out of shape is no reason to compare him unfavorably with the photograph, which would be a better portrait without the distortion.

While we may gain from a photograph a concept of how a dog should appear standing, his structure and proportions, yet, we must emphasize that his structure is no better than the use he makes of it. We must see the dog in action to arrive at a true evaluation of him.

For this we require a considerable space, a straightaway of 100 feet or even more. The small judging rings in too many dog show hamper the judging of this particular breed, which is evaluated particularly upon its gait. In a small ring the judge is able, because he must, to make his decisions between exhibits in which there is considerable disparity. It is impossible in small space to make a complete evaluation of a dog in action, as it is also impossible to arrive at an accurate comparative decision between two or more evenly matched exhibits.

Gait

In our examination of the dog we shall take into account a powerful rear action, whether we shall find it or not. If it is lacking, it may still be possible to win at indoor shows or those with limited ring space. However, we have ample room for our examination and without a powerful drive our German Shepherd is somewhat short of perfection.

Let us proceed to the consideration of the dog's manner of going.

Standing directly behind the dog, have the assistant walk the animal away in front of you, turn directly around and walk toward you. In this part of the examination, the dog is not called upon to exert himself. The trueness of his action is all that we are seeking to observe. Are his hocks parallel one to the other, as they should be? Or is there some evidence of cowhocks or of bandy legs? Are the hindquarters trussed or spraddled out? Or are they possibly so close together as to interfere? These are seen as the dog moves away. As he returns, note the parallelism of the front legs. Are the front legs so tightly attached to the shoulders as to cause them to cross or weave or even to tend to do so? On the other hand, are they so loosely attached as to cause the dog to paddle like a side-wheeler? One is as bad as the other. If he "frenches" while standing, it is impossible for him to move without throwing his feet sidewise, but this is not the same movement as looseness of shoulder in which the whole body lurches from side to side, supporting the weight first on one side and then on the other.

177

These tests are for ordinary soundness and can be made in a comparatively small space. Unless he possesses an ordinary or garden variety of soundness, a dog cannot be expected to perform well at more rapid gaits.

There are of course degrees of soundness. While we may desire it to be absolute, a dog may deviate slightly from being perfectly sound without condemnation. It is better that he exhibit several such minute deviations than a single gross one. A trace of cow-hocks plus a trace of looseness of shoulder is to be preferred to gross cow-hocks. Or a very slight spraddle plus a trace of frenchiness is to be preferred to a badly frenched front. It is hardly to be anticipated that perfection will be found in any part, although it may be. It is better to find numerous minute and hardly noticeable faults than a single bad one. The analogy of the engine again applies: a machine may function fairly well with numerous small maladjustments, whereas another machine perfect in all its parts but one and that one part grossly wrong may function very badly or not at all.

In order to see these features, it is necessary that the dog be moved at a moderate fast trot, which is best seen from the dog's side. Stand well back from his path and have him moved with enough freedom to lower his head, if he desires to do so and if he needs to preserve his balance with his neck. The further away from him you stand, the better you can observe him.

Note whether his stride is long and flexible, as it should be, or short and choppy, wasteful of motion and of energy. A dog properly angulated, fore and aft, will extend his hind leg far under his body, grasp the floor (or better the earth) firmly, and, extending his leg in a powerful follow through, throw the distance between him. The power thus generated is transmitted through the spine to the shoulder, which, if properly angulated, opens to compensate for the long rear stride with an equally long stride in front.

There is little purpose in ample angulation in the rear, however well used it may be, if the angle at the points of the shoulder is not sufficient to absorb the stride. It is equally futile to possess great angulation of shoulder without ample angulation in the rear and ample use of it to produce the power for transmission. A moderate and equalized angulation both aft and before is to be preferred to perfect hindquarters with an upright shoulder or to a perfect shoulder with inadequate hindquarters. Of course we want perfection of both ends of the dog, as open a shoulder as possible and as much angulation of hindquarters as the musculature can support. Excessive rear angulation without the muscles to support and articulate it results in weakness. The rear angulation is merely a series of long levers that will fall together without muscular tension.

The loss of their powerful stride in our modern dogs is due to a loss of the muscular power to propel the dog, and a prevalence of straight

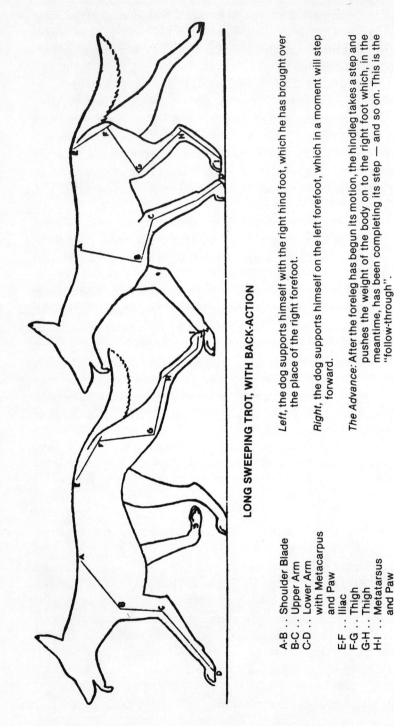

LONG SWEEPING TROT, WITH BACK-ACTION

Left, the dog supports himself with the right hind foot, which he has brought over the place of the right forefoot.

Right, the dog supports himself on the left forefoot, which in a moment will step forward.

The Advance: After the foreleg has begun its motion, the hindleg takes a step and pushes the weight of the body on to the right foot which, in the meantime, has been completing its step — and so on. This is the "follow-through".

A-B .. Shoulder Blade
B-C .. Upper Arm
C-D .. Lower Arm
with Metacarpus
and Paw
E-F .. Iliac
F-G .. Thigh
G-H .. Thigh
H-I .. Metatarsus
and Paw

shoulders. It is not due to a loss of *rear* angulation. There are more well-angled dogs and dogs with better angulation than in the early heyday of superb movers; they have simply lost their ability to utilize the rear angulation they possess. Some dogs with sufficient front and rear angulation also lack the driving power required. This leaves us open to the doubt that the action of the breed has actually deteriorated. We may well ask ourselves whether our current crop of dogs is receiving the exercise, especially in their puppyhood, to develop the muscles of their hindquarters to carry them over the ground with the agility and power their great-grandfathers displayed. Conditioning is all-important.

The stride of the forequarters should be as long as the stride behind, else at every trotting step the amount of the difference in those lengths will be lost. This is best seen from standing back a considerable way from the dog and having him led past one at a trot. The exact length of the over-step, as it is called, can be ascertained by sprinkling a thin layer of powder, flour, or even fine sand over the dog's path to obtain footprints and measuring the distance by which the rear stride exceeds the front stride. There should be no difference in these measurements.

High, hackney-like action of the front feet is often mistakenly admired, being assumed to give the dog style. It is usually accompanied by a high carriage of the head. It results in waste of effort and is not at all desirable. It is not, however, so bad a fault as the excessive lifting of the hind leg in its forward thrust. This last is exceedingly wasteful of energy, serves no useful purpose whatever, and is awkward. It may occur in either leg or both legs, and gives the impression of string halt.

In action, the feet should just fairly clear the ground without any semblance of dragging. This conservation of energy may appear futile, when it is realized that the dog wastes so much energy in play and in useless activity; but in emergency in herding (or even in police service) the German Shepherd Dog is called upon to cover ground with the greatest celerity and to display tremendous endurance and stamina. In evaluating the merits of a dog, it becomes necessary to consider him in relation to the greatest exertion a member of the breed will ever be called upon to make. It is not enough that he can rather easily perform all the tasks you are likely to demand of him; but to be a typical specimen of his breed he must be structurally fit for intense and arduous service.

In fast trot, the dog should stretch out, with back entirely level and without undulation. His movement should be long, lithe, and powerful, and with no apparent effort. He should skim the ground

181

with his feet. The best gait is not light or feathery, but the step should be firm, throwing the ground behind him. The tail may be raised to or beyond the horizontal, but it should not attain a vertical position or be turned over the back. It need not be perceptibly raised at all. This fast trot is the final test of the dog's worth. If the gait is correct, the structure of the skeleton needs must be correct.

Style

A German Shepherd Dog is theoretically merely a machine for herding sheep. What contributes to his efficiency as a herding dog makes for excellence, and whatever detracts from his herding ability is deemed a fault. This utilitarian theory is essentially true, and it is adhered to (or was prior to the war) in Germany, the homeland of the breed. Nobility, beauty, pride were merely fortuitous attributes, and the personality of the dog counted little in German shows.

The Americans, however, demand class in their dogs, class plus conformation to a standard. A plain dog correctly constructed may get by to a high position in an award list, but such a dog is not great. A great dog must be a noble dog, beautiful and aware of his own beauty, a dominant personality. Even animals can project "star" quality. Style, flourish, elan may in an American show carry a dog further than perfect structure. A great dog of the breed must be endowed with an indefinable divine spark.

However much style and personality a dog may possess, they can never rightly take the place of correct conformation and gait; but when they are superimposed upon conformation and gait they make for greatness.

Evaluation of Faults

The novice fancier of the German Shepherd Dog must be warned on the one hand against the condemnation of his dog for some minor and minute fault. On the other hand, he must not seek to condone a major fault and deceive himself. There are no perfect dogs, and perfection must not be anticipated in any dog. Especially shall he not attach too much importance to faults that can be remedied. Fatness or thinness is not so much the fault of the dog as of the keeper. A fat dog may be reduced in weight, or a thin one may be fattened. The possession of

Stylish German Shepherd Dog bitch, Ch. Amber a.d. Edelheim, owned by Joan Ortigara.

A typy bitch, Ch. Valmy's Uncola, owned by Charles Mardecz.

Ch. Orpha of Edgetowne, honorary ROM Dam, in whelp. Note beautiful structure.

the correct coat at a given time is less important (except in an actual show) than his known ability to grow a correct coat. Of course, for formal exhibition it is necessary that the dog be set down with a full bloom of coat, but for informal examination the certainty that he can grow a coat, irrespective of its present condition, is all that is required. This certainty is predicated upon the fact that the dog has at some previous time had a correct coat with a full undercoat. If he has grown a coat, he can grow one again. Neither should a dog be penalized in this examination for softness or flabbiness of musculature, which can be hardened with judicious exercise. A flabby dog in a show is almost certain to go down to defeat, but it has nothing to do with his fundamental merits, which we are here seeking to ascertain.

But the pride of ownership should not prompt us to forgive obvious faults. A square body, stilty hindlegs, an upright shoulder, a crooked front, a weak back, cow-hocks, an awkward gait, any of these faults, if pronounced, seriously handicap a dog in competition. In fact, dogs that evince such faults should not be exhibited at all. It is necessary to forget that he is your dog and to look at him objectively. Charge against him all his shortcomings, but don't make mountains out of mole-hills. He may be a good pal and able to perform all that is required of him without being a first rate show specimen. Accept him for what he is, and do not expect too much from him. A woman may be good-looking and presentable without aspiring to be a moving picture star.

Above all, consider the dog as a unit. Symmetry and balance of the whole organism are more important than any of the individual parts. There is a general disposition, especially among fanciers of German Shepherd Dogs, so to analyze dogs, to take them apart and judge the pieces, that the dog as a whole, the ensemble, is lost sight of. It is only as the individual parts fit together to make a complete organism that the whole dog is good or bad or mediocre.

However excellent any part may be, if it is too large or too small to mesh together with the other parts, the dog is thrown out of balance and his symmetry is lost. It is often said that if it were possible to take some parts of one dog and other parts from another and make a composite dog we should achieve perfection. Aside from the fact that it is impossible to do so, the parts would not fit together. The dog is a unit.

It is the recognition of that unity that enables the experienced judge to evaluate the merits of a dog in so short a time. He sees the animal as a whole. When a class of dogs enters the ring and parades before him, he is able to arrive at a concept of which dogs are to win, which are to be discarded. He looks for balance and symmetry. Of course his opinion must be confirmed or denied by closer examination, but it is usually confirmed. No such instant evaluation of a dog is to be expected of the amateur fancier. He must examine the individual parts to know why his dog is good or bad; but, having examined the parts, he must fit them together into a whole dog. And the whole is greater than any of its parts. If the dog has symmetry and balance, it is a good dog; and if it lacks symmetry or balance it is not so good, no matter how excellent the individual pieces of dog that make up the whole may be.

There is little difference between the sexes in this particular breed. Bitches as a rule have more quality and refinement than dogs, somewhat less bone in proportion to their size, and are usually somewhat smaller. However, a large bitch may be slightly larger than a small dog. The dog is usually more arched of neck, more stallion-like. Size, within accepted limits, is a matter of little consideration.

We sometimes see a dog that in make and shape is more fitted to be a bitch; and we sometimes see a big, slashing, aggressive bitch upon which we could graft male organs. A first rate dog should conform to the character of its sex. Dogginess in a bitch, or bitchiness in a dog is a minor fault, and is subject to some penalty.

185

Canadian Grand Victor, Am. and Can. Ch. Ulk Wikingerblut, SchH III, A.D., CACIB, R.O.M. (1956-1968), pictured with the fruits of his sensational winning. One of the great Shepherd showmen of all time with an overall record (U.S. and Canada) of 128 Bests of Breed, 50 Group Firsts and 28 Bests of Show. During his show career Ulk travelled over 200,000 air miles and competed in 38 states, always handled by his co-owner, Mary Roberts.

7

Character of the
German Shepherd Dog

"The German Shepherd Dog should possess firmness of nerves, attentiveness, imperturbable nature, watchfulness, loyalty and incorruptibility, in addition to courage, fighting spirit, and aggressiveness when required. These traits make him outstanding as a Working Dog in general, and in particular as a Watch Dog, Guide Dog, Protection Dog, Tracking Dog"
— Quoted from the standard of the *Deutches Schäferhunde.*

A working dog is one belonging to a breed that is physically and mentally capable of carrying out particular duties. Included in the classification of working dogs are many breeds that are no longer required to perform the functions for which they were intended. The German Shepherd Dog, however, since it was first developed, has continued to serve mankind in many capacities.

Sincere, dedicated breeders throughout the world have maintained and improved upon the structure of the agile, handy, trotting dog used for herding, and have developed the mental characteristics necessary for stability and trainability. Over eighty years of selection, weeding out the dull, the vicious, and the timid, has resulted in a breed of superb intelligence.

A dog for all seasons.

Companion and Guardian. GV Red Rock's Gino, CD, ROM, was evidence that a top showdog, obedience performer and fine sire could also be a family dog.

German Shepherd Dogs are in nearly every country of the world, and the breed has become nearly synonymous with intelligence. Unfortunately, we find outside of Germany that many breeders place too little emphasis on what is in the head. Their obsession with beauty leaves some breeders only handsome conformation specimens with "feathers in their heads". Empty-headedness is sad enough, but timidity or viciousness are even worse.

A German Shepherd Dog should be self-confident, poised, eager, alert, and willing to make friends—unless it has been specially trained not to do so. It should *never* be timid, nervous, tail-tucking, looking for spooks in the air, or aggressive without provocation.

Which category does your dog fall into? If the first, you have a good start. If the latter, you have our sympathy, and you should look for a good veterinarian to painlessly dispose of him. A dog with bad temperament is a nuisance and a hazard. When there are so many attractive German Shepherd Dogs available, don't settle for a condition that can bring only trouble and heartache. Recent studies by the United States Health Department have placed dog bites in the millions each year. A shy dog is just as prone to bite as a vicious one, so don't harbor either.

Temperament

Adaption to the environment is most necessary for the full development of the dog whether it be a guard dog or family pet. Varied temperaments are required in varied uses of the breed, but basically the ideal dog is adaptable to its situation and must be mentally sound to perform its role.

In an effort to assist its members in weeding out undesirable temperament, the German Shepherd Dog Club of America in 1980 adopted a Temperament Evaluation Test, administered throughout the United States by approved testers. Dogs passing this test will be awarded a Temperament Certificate, and the "T.C." identification of it can be affixed to their names as are other earned titles.

The test is based upon one adopted by the Doberman Pinscher Club of America under the leadership of Vic Monteleon. In it, dogs are graded on their reactions to the following:

1. *The Neutral Stranger.* In this first test, the dog is to show no fear of the non-threatening stranger, who ignores him completely; however, if the dog tries to make up to the stranger, it is considered a plus.

Joyful worker! Ch. Bero of Bihari, UDT,
owned by Klaus Elfert.

Am. and Can. Ch. Wynthea's Tillie, Am. & Can. UDT,
owned and handled by Mrs. Freeman Spencer, Jr.

2. *The Friendly Stranger.* This time the stranger tries to coax the dog over to be petted and the handler may encourage the dog to be friendly in return.
3. *Reaction to Noise—Hidden Clattering Alert and Investigation.* The assistant is hidden out of sight on the tailgate of a wagon or van, and as the handler and dog approach, he rattles a can full of stones. The dog must be willing to investigate and sniff at the can.
4. *Gunshots.* Several shots from a .22 caliber athletic starter pistol are fired into the air five yards away from the dog. The dog may startle at first but must recover and not show fear. It is fine if he moves toward the shots.
5. *Reaction to Visual Stimuli—The Umbrella Test.* A spring-loaded black umbrella is opened by an assistant who is sitting in a lawn chair. This is done when the dog is nine feet from the tip of the umbrella, which is raised slowly and pointed at the dog. The dog must move forward (with encouragement if necessary) to investigate, although he does not have to touch it to pass the test.
6. *Footing test.* The dog must demonstrate a willingness to walk the length of a black Polyethylene strip of 16 feet and he must do this on a loose lead without trying to jump on and off it. He must then walk the length of a wire mesh exercise pen that has been unfolded and lays flat on the ground.
7. *The threat test.* This last test is an important one and is in three parts. First, a staggering, spinning weird looking and sounding person crosses the dog's path at about 20 feet. This man, who is dressed in a long raincoat and floppy hat, is not yet directing his behavior at the dog. In the second part, the stranger continues his weird behavior, but starts approaching the dog. In the third part, his behavior turns to threatening motions toward the dog with a stick in his upraised hand. The dog is then expected to show aggression toward this threat.

This program is, of course, still in its infancy and more challenging tests no doubt will be developed. But even in its simplest form, a Temperament Test requires an owner to devote time for personal attention and socialization (much needed by our breed).

Obedience Training

"A mind is a terrible thing to waste," says the TV promo. Naturally the reference is to human gray matter, but it is shameful also to neglect the intelligence and trainability of a German Shepherd Dog.

If you want to have an unhappy, often troublesome child, neglect his training; give him little or no guidelines of accepted behavior and leave him to his own devices. Similarly, if you neglect a dog, you are in for some rough times. Left on his own, an intelligent dog will find ways to employ his energies and the results can be TROUBLE.

Assuming that you have a dog of acceptable temperament and wish to enjoy his companionship to the utmost, the best investment you can make is to attend an obedience training school. If there is none in

German Shepherd Dog doing the long jump (9 feet) at Crystal Palace Dog Trial in England in 1932.

German Shepherd Dogs were in the forefront of Obedience development in America. At this 193 training class in California, they typically outnumbered the other breeds.

your area, then purchase a good book on the subject and at least give your dog the basic training needed to make a good citizen of him. Remember always that the German Shepherd Dog is a family dog, not a kennel dog. He craves and thrives on human companionship, and is willing to learn whatever you offer in training.

The companionship and devotion of a handsome, intelligent, well-trained German Shepherd Dog will bring rewards that are unique in dogdom. Once you have owned a good one, no dog of another breed can supplant him.

Dog training is not new. Owners have trained dogs for centuries, but methods were not uniform. Late in the 1800s, organized training clubs began to appear in Europe, and after the turn of the century the S.V. in Germany had organized Schutzhund Trials.

By the 1920s there were a number of professional trainers (primarily of German Shepherd Dogs and Doberman Pinschers) in America who would train a dog for its owner, or give the owner lessons in handling behavior problems. Owners trained in groups, gave exhibitions and competed in trials, but these were confined to working breeds. One trainer wrote of having attended an Obedience and Police Dog trial at Staten Island in New York as early in 1916. And Obedience trials for German Shepherd Dogs (at that time they were called field trials) were held in 1923 and 1924 by the Alsatian Shepherd Dog Club of Canada, later to become the German Shepherd Dog Club of Canada.

But formal Obedience, as we know it today in America, had its roots in England where, by the 1930s, tests with specific rules were being held for all breeds under the sponsorship of the Associated Sheep, Police, Army Dog Society (the ASPADS). These tests were the inspiration and model for the original Obedience tests drawn up on this side of the Atlantic by Mrs. Whitehouse Walker and Miss Blanche Saunders.

Mrs. Walker, a successful Poodle exhibitor, felt that showing off a dog's beauty and structure at a dog show presented but one aspect of a breed, and she saw Obedience competition as a way to demonstrate the dog's intelligence. Together with Miss Saunders, she encouraged several Eastern clubs to put on Obedience tests along with their conformation shows, and campaigned to have the American Kennel Club take over active control. In March 1936 the AKC Board of Directors officially approved the concept.

Aided by Josef Weber, a professional trainer who was also a key personality in the beginnings of the Seeing Eye, Mrs. Walker and Miss

Am. & Can. Ch. Anthony of Cosalta, first champion German Shepherd Dog to earn the CDX degree. Owned by Miss Marie J. Leary.

Marie Leary early promoted the ideal of dogs with both conformation and Obedience titles. Pictured, l. r. are, Ch. Nox, CD; Ch. Marc, CD; Ch. Jessica, CD; Ch. Lance, CD; Ch. Luana, CD; and Ch. Craig, CD—of Cosalta, Miss Leary's kennel prefix.

Saunders formulated rules and regulations, and the first AKC-licensed test was held at the North Westchester Kennel Club show at Mt. Kisco, New York, in June 1936.

German Shepherd Dogs have been outstanding in Obedience right from the start. Ch. Schwarzpels von Mardex, owned by Walter P. Phieffer, was one of the first two dogs to earn all the Obedience degrees. He completed his U.D. (Utility Dog) title by winning the first Tracking Test held under AKC rules, judged by Josef Weber. Marie Leary trained many dogs to degrees in early Obedience days, including Am. & Can. Ch. Anthony of Cosalta, the first champion German Shepherd Dog to earn a C.D.X. (Companion Dog Excellent).

In the beginning bench show exhibitors looked upon Obedience as a fad, but determined enthusiasts persisted. The two resolute pioneers, Mrs. Walker and Miss Saunders, travelled over 10,000 miles promoting their methods of training and demonstrating how easily good manners could be taught.

Many local kennel clubs originally were reluctant to accept Obedience Trials as part of the dog show scene, treating it like a much-disliked step-child if they bothered with it at all. Having founded the Lancaster Dog Training Club in 1945, this author remembers the handicaps Obedience enthusiasts encountered early in its history. Now Obedience Trials are an outstanding feature of most American Kennel Club licensed shows where the general public can enjoy excellent performance of well-trained dogs. Often spectators are amazed at the display of intelligence and willingness to respond. This is part of a dog show they can understand and relate to.

The German Shepherd Dog has always been one of the top breeds in degrees earned. Many breeders show in breed classes *and* Obedience. The German Shepherd Dog Club of America awards medals and plaques to members who earn American Kennel Club titles. The club presents the Obedience Victor or Victrix trophy at its annual Specialty Show and encourages Regional Clubs to conduct training classes for conformation showing and Obedience Trials.

There are hundreds of training clubs and privately run classes available. Anyone can avail himself of expert advice in making his dog a good citizen and maybe a blue ribbon winner.

Training should be fun for both handler and dog, and the companionship between a dog and his owner can be so beautiful. Dogs can be trained with kindness, quiet patience and much affection. Avoid the loud harsh methods some trainers apply, for they are not necessary. Firmness need not be severity. Brow-beating shows a deplorable lack of understanding of how joyful dog ownership can be.

Because we feel training your dog and, if possible, earning at least a Companion Dog degree is very important, we include an outline of current requirements for Obedience titles. It is quoted, with permission, from the AKC's official book, *The Complete Dog Book*.

Obedience trials are tests of man and dog. In Obedience, the dog must perform a prescribed set of exercises which the judge grades or—as it is called by Obedience enthusiasts—scores. The dog's conformation has no bearing on its being able to compete in Obedience. Dogs that would be disqualified from the show ring under a breed standard, even spayed bitches and neutered dogs, may compete in Obedience trials.

Obedience is divided into three levels, each more difficult than the preceding one. At each level a competitor is working for an AKC Obedience degree or title. The three levels and titles are:

Novice—Companion Dog (C.D.)

Open—Companion Dog Excellent (C.D.X.)

Utility—Utility Dog (U.D.)

Novice work embraces the basics that all dogs should be taught to make them good companions. The six exercises in Novice work are: heel on leash, stand for examination, heel free, recall, long sit and long down. *Open* work consists of seven exercises: heel free, drop on recall, retrieve on flat, retrieve over the high jump, broad jump, long sit and long run. *Utility* work consists of: signal exercise, two scent discrimination tests, directed retrieve, directed jumping and group examination.

To receive an Obedience title a dog must earn three "legs." To get credit for a leg, a dog must score at least 170 points out of a possible 200 (the passing score and grand total are the same at each level, although the exercises vary) and get more than fifty percent on each exercise.

In addition, dogs can earn titles at official tracking tests held under AKC tules. These titles are at two levels:

Tracking Dog (T.D.)

Tracking Dog Excellent (T.D.X.)

A relatively new title that dogs in Obedience can earn is Obedience Trial Champion (O.T. Ch.). Only dogs that have earned the Utility Dog title can earn points toward an Obedience Trial Championship. Championship points are recorded for dogs earning a First or Second place in Open B or Utility Class (or Utility B, if divided) according to the schedule of points established by the AKC Board of Directors To become an Obedience Trial Champion a dog must win 100 points that include a First place in Utility (or Utility B, if divided) with at least

3 dogs in competition, a First place in Open B with at least 6 dogs in competition and a third First place in either of these competitions. The three First places must be won under three different judges.

The Versatility Class is an extra class that combines two exercises from Novice, Open and Utility. This is a fun class with no credit except prizes at the Trial.

A number of clubs are training dogs in Scent-Hurdle races. This competitive sport is exciting to watch and demonstrates that even our dogs enjoy "just showing off." Each year the German Shepherd Dog Club of America sets aside time at the National Specialty for Scent-Hurdle racing. Usually four teams are in competition from Regional Clubs and these teams afford some exciting moments.

It is possible to train your own dog without benefit of class or trainer. However, there are about 1200 cities where classes are available. If there is a kennel club show in your town or a German Shepherd Dog Specialty Show, attend it and inquire about training facilities. Complete rules and regulations can be obtained from the American Kennel Club at 51 Madison Avenue, New York, N.Y. 10010.

Schutzhund (Protection Dog) Training

In the past few years, proponents of the German concept of Obedience training have encouraged Schutzhund training throughout the world. Of several organizations in the United States, only the United Schutzhund Club of America utilizes S.V. rules and S.V. judges in their trials.

In 1980, 250 titles were earned by dogs in the United States under these rules.

Max von Stephanitz, given credit for so much of the breed's early development, was responsible also for setting down basic rules for training in absolute obedience, protection of owner and property, and tracking. His fundamental premise of the breed's potentials have been developed into the Schutzhund phase of training.

At present there are no American Kennel Club events at which Schutzhund Trials are officially sanctioned, and AKC recognition is not foreseeable in the near future. In the United States, Obedience Trial rules permit participation by all breeds, whereas Schutzhund Trials must, by their very nature, be limited to the larger working breeds. Since it is a function limited to so few breeds, it is not firmly established in this country. Because of this and because it presents a possible hazard to the general public, the American Kennel Club has been taking a cautious approach to involvement.

Schutzhund training.—*Narlesky*

Goals of Schutzhund training, with three degrees attainable (SchH I, SchH II, and SchH III) and an advanced tracking degree (F.H.), are to produce an obedient, courageous dog that will protect. Unfortunately, the term "protection dog" is translated to "attack dog" by the uninformed and so the movement has gained unwarranted criticism at times. Schutzhund dogs are not trained in the same manner as guard dogs nor should they be identified as "attack dogs." There is a question troubling many breeders in this country, a question posed by Josef Weber as early as the 1940s, as to why a protection-trained dog is needed as a family pet. The dog is trained to protect through powerful biting and from puppyhood, a dog destined for Schutzhund work is given encouragement to develop his innate instincts. If a dog so trained is handled by a trainer-owner who is on top of the dog at all times, there is no hazard involved. However, it is of utmost importance that this "dog sport" be in the hands of competent trainers and that only dogs of sound disposition be trained.

The AKC rules for Obedience Trials and the S.V. rules for Schutzhund parallel each other in many instances. However, there are also many differences; the Schutzhund exercises are more difficult and present more challenges to dog and handler. They can be used to develop fully the traits so admired in the breed, i.e., courage, willingness, to obey, loyalty, intelligence, trainability. Properly applied, this training can help eliminate undesirable qualities in the breed by weeding out animals which do not measure up to criteria for a Schutzhund trained dog. This training *never* should be used to cover up bad traits.

Each year the United Schutzhund Club will be entering a team at the European Schutzhund Championship Trials. To date, teams from this country have given excellent performances and, as expertise improves, teams from this country should equal any in the world.

Handsome is as handsome does—Ch. Ingo of LaSalle. Jack Sinykin became interested in training guide dogs for the blind as early as 1925. The famous Master Eye Foundation school he established in Minnesota was founded on dogs out of his own LaSalle Kennels.

8

The Most Utilitarian
Dog of All

THE GERMAN SHEPHERD DOG, as its name implies, was developed as a herder and guardian of sheep. As we learned early in this book, after the need for protecting sheep diminished, the breed's sponsors looked to other areas in which this highly intelligent animal could serve mankind.

For many years, the German Shepherd Dog has borne the stigma of viciousness because of his great courage and instinct for protection. His character made him ideal for police and guard work. After 75 years, he is still number one in this service throughout the world.

Protection Dog

Guarding property, whether as an employed canine or a family pet, comes readily to a sane, sensible German Shepherd Dog. When a property is so guarded, any individual should be cautious of challenging the protection dog. *Well-trained* dogs know when they are on duty, but unless they are set free to roam a property and guard at will, they do not "attack" unless ordered to do so. However, they may, and should, *hold* a suspicious visitor either by softly gripping a leg or cornering by threatening barks until relieved by command of the handler or owner.

Schutzhund training is discussed in the chapter on Character; this training by private individuals of protective pets can be a mixed blessing, for here, too, the public stresses the attack aspect far more than necessary.

Deputy Danny Goodrich of the San Diego Sheriff's office, watches his dog Chief go over the 4-feet high chain link fence under the observation of Senior Judge Captain Arthur J. Haggerty (right) at the First Annual Police Dog Trials held in Burlingame, California. Deputy Goodrich and Chief took top honors with 491.6 out of a possible 500 points.

140 PAIRS OF BOOTS WERE ORDERED FROM A NEW ZEALAND BOOTMAKER FOR 70 GERMAN SHEPHERDS ON COUNTRY'S POLICE FORCE. BOOTS PROTECT DOGS' FEET DURING "HAZARDOUS TOURS OF DUTY"

—courtesy, *Gaines Dog Research Center.*

Police Dog

When we came into the breed in the 1930s, the German Shepherd Dog was still being called "police dog" by the general public and many dog fanciers. Early on, the distinguished John Gans advised us that the best way to explain away the nisnomer was to ask, "Are all Irishmen policemen because many policemen are Irish?"

The reputation of the police work done in Germany preceded the breed's entry here. However, it was not used extensively in this capacity in the United States until after World War II. Now many large metropolitan police forces, and sheriffs' offices in remote areas, rely upon the psychological deterrent a police dog provides.

A typical instance is that of a Baltimore dog and patrolman team called upon to check on a prowler in a warehouse. The team had the culprit tracked to the second floor landing, when he jumped out of the window. His reasoning—he'd rather break his bones than have the dog "get him."

Many a lone foot patrolman or radio-car patrolman can rely on his hairy companion as an extra pair of eyes and ears. Alertness and fidelity have endeared this breed to the uniformed handler, so many forces find it advantageous to have the dog remain with the policeman as a house dog, rather than kenneling it. The dog changes as readily to a pet when off-duty as the policeman becomes a civilian.

In 1979, Samuel G. Chapman recorded 349 enforcement agencies in the United States using dogs. One of the most celebrated has been the Philadelphia Canine Corps, established for over 20 years. A 1977 article in *The Canine Graphic* stated that 102 dogs were on daily police duty in the subways, airports, parks and streets of Philadelphia. Of these, 98% were German Shepherd Dogs, chosen (according to the head of the Corps) because "they have proven to be the breed most fitted to the job—strong and aggressive, but not overly ferocious."

The article reported on how handler and dog are trained as a team, repeatedly drilled in control and self-control as they become familiar with each other. The training period covers 14 weeks. Early emphasis is on Obedience work and at end of the training, the dogs are tested for completion of all AKC Obedience skills. The Corps maintains an obstacle course where dogs are trained to climb ladders and stairs and scale walls as high as six or seven feet. The dogs must be agile enough to jump through windows, climb barrels, walk and balance themselves on thin widths, and clear over 10 feet in broad jumping.

Attack work is not introduced until the sixth week of training. The dog is taught restraint, but if the handler is struck by his suspect, the dog will attack and apprehend. When on car patrol, the dog is taught to exit the vehicle and advance to the handler's side in situations of danger. Should there be gunfire, the dog will unhesitantly attack and subdue the criminal.

There is strong emphasis on scent training, not only for bomb and narcotic detection, but also for locating guns, bullet casings, knives, etc. for evidence.

The New York City Police Department was one of the earliest (in 1907) to employ dogs. In recent years, New York has successfully used policeman/dog teams to patrol the subways. And in 1981, German Shepherd Dogs were positioned at a storage yard for subway cars as a deterrent to grafitti artists. This has proven most effective — at last report, trains were untouched and not a single can of paint was found in the yard policed by the dog.

Dogs have proved very valuable to policemen as a psychological deterrent in crowd control, too. However much some groups might deplore their use in this, it would seem preferable to having to resort to mace or water from high-powered hoses. A dog is highly visible, so that rioters, looters, or dangerous threatening crowds can be forewarned and respond sensibly with no physical harm.

Bomb Detector Dogs

Picture yourself travelling non-stop from New York to Los Angeles when an unscheduled landing is made at Pittsburgh, Pa. Upon disembarking you observe two uniformed men and two extremely alert German Shepherd Dogs boarding the empty plane. "Aha," a fellow passenger remarks, "must be a bomb on board."

At airports over the world — at thirty in the United States — two teams of dog and handler are available. In this country the Federal Aviation Administration selects airports for this service so that no plane, having received a bomb threat, is more than thirty minutes flying time away from the keen nose of a bomb detector dog. The public will never know how many lives and how much property these highly trained dogs have saved. One life saved repays the expense involved.

In a program initially begun in 1972, dogs — mainly German Shepherd Dogs — trained by the Air Force at Lackland, Texas, under

Up, up and over. Dog being trained for work with the Delaware State Police.

The German Shepherd Dog's strong sense of smell can solve problems in heavy cover. — Photo, with permission, from *"The Koehler Method of Guard Dog Training"*, copyright, Howell Book House.

U.S. CUSTOMS DOG FANG DISCOVERED $3.5 MILLION IN MARIJUANA, IN TWO TRUCKS AT MEXICO-U.S. BORDER BURIED UNDER 16 TONS OF ONIONS!

—courtesy, *Gaines Dog Research Center.*

The Australian Bureau of Customs uses German Shepherd Dogs for combatting smuggling, too. Picture is of a customs officer and his dog checking luggage at Kingsford Smith Airport at Sydney. Each dog is assigned to an experienced customs officer and regular patrols are made of airports, wharves, warehouses, bond stores, etc. The dogs have proved remarkably effective, finding drugs in such places as sealed tins of food, inside linings of tape cassettes and in water tanks of camper vans.

206

the co-sponsorship of the Federal Aviation Administration and the Civil Aviation Security Service, have helped secure the safety of airports and planes. It takes 21 weeks to train dog and handler at Lackland. Then, after two weeks of on-the-site (airport) training, the team is ready. In one recent test of capability and accuracy, 371 samples of explosives were hidden in spots not known to the handler. Every imaginable and improbable spot was chosen in terminals, planes, cargo areas, parking lots. 360 finds were made, the inaccuracy mainly due to one team's misses.

According to an FAA administrator, "Technology has not been able yet to come up with a mechanical 'sniffer' that can compete with the nose of a trained dog. . . . ." The advantages are many. The dog can detect minute amounts of explosive, search more efficiently without disturbing cartons or containers (thus decreasing risk of detonating devices) and work more rapidly in situations where time is important, and he expects no more than shelter, food and a pat on the head for his accomplishments.

The bomb detector dogs are loaned out in the metropolitan areas near airports and have been highly successful when called upon in this time of terrorist threat and just garden variety kooks, security forces have turned to dogs to search out their weapons—bombs.

Drug Detector Dogs

Another service that dogs perform in our complex and crime-ridden society is that of the Drug Detector Dog. This group is under the control of the Department of the Treasury and U.S. Customs Service Detector Dog Training Program. Here, too, the German Shepherd Dog is preferred because of his "super sniffer," courage, intelligence and versatility. The program has been acclaimed throughout the world and has been copied by many countries to help control the horrendous traffic in drugs. As an example, "Bub," the first to retire from the service, was responsible for 250 seizures and detection of over 14 tons of marijuana in less than two years.

Narcotic dogs are used at main ports of entry where they can check out a vehicle in one minute as opposed to an agent's required twenty minutes. In thirty minutes a dog can search for drugs in four hundred to five hundred packages; an agent would need at least two days. On cargo docks, airport terminals, international mail distribution centers, dogs consistently are alerted to contraband and serve as the smugglers' worst enemies.

In spite of ingenious camouflage methods, the flow of narcotics into the United States is significantly halted when a sniffing dog is at work. Freshly painted bags, perfume, talcum powder, raw onions, onions, onion juice, hollowed out cheese, chocolate coating, all have been used but the hiding places were discovered. Finds have been made in gas tanks, ceramic statues, metal tubing, hollow tables, shoe soles and leather bags.

Current statistics for the U.S. Customs' dope-detectors are particularly impressive when looked at for the return the government gets for its small investment in training.

Unfortunately, it has been necessary to employ Narcotics Detector Drugs on American military bases here and abroad. The first unit was at Homestead Air Force Base in 1969 and dogs now are deployed in many areas where smuggling in of narcotics has become a problem.

At the end of the Vietnam War, military dog team veterans were retrained for customs work. The versatility of the German Shepherd Dog made the changes in training and service possible.

This exceptional canine capability is being explored for utilization also by industry. For example, oil companies are employing dogs to find underground leaks; gas lines are regularly patrolled in some areas; mine tunnels can be pre-checked for gas; and, of course, we have seen the guard dog on duty at many commercial sites.

Guide Dog

As early as 1819, an Austrian priest suggested that a dog in rigid harness could be trained to guide the blind. In the early 1920s this method was employed at Potsdam where Germany was training dogs for war blinded veterans. At that time, Dorothy Eustis, engaged in training dogs for police and Red Cross work, maintained her extensive Fortunate Fields kennel near Vevey in the Swiss Alps, where her main interest was in developing a strain of dogs with great stamina and intelligence. Her assistant was Elliot "Jack" Humphrey, horse trainer and breeder, who had a deep interest in the genetics of German Shepherd Dogs.

When Mrs. Eustis wrote an article for *The Saturday Evening Post* about guide dogs, it attracted the attention of a blind Nashville youth, Morris Frank, who requested a dog for himself. After making the trip, alone, to Switzerland, this nineteen-year old returned to the United States with the famous Buddy—forerunner of the Seeing Eye, Inc. With great enthusiasm and support from Mrs. Eustis he started a

Narcotic Detector Dogs in U.S. Customs' service.

An early graduate leaving with his guide dog from the world-famous Seeing Eye school at Morristown, N.J. Thousands of German Shepherd Dogs have been thus trained since the inception of the school over fifty years ago.

school in Nashville in 1929 with Josef Weber as trainer, moving it to Morristown, New Jersey in 1931 where the Seeing Eye, Inc., has flourished as a model institution. 7500 dogs have been placed to date and, together with three other outstanding schools, Guide Dogs for the Blind, Leader Dogs, and Guiding Eyes for the Blind, over 800 dogs are trained annually. Other schools throughout the U.S. successfully train German Shepherd Dogs for their greatest contribution to mankind—helping sightless enter the mainstream of society.

In 1925, Jack Sinykin had become interested in the German program for the sightless. The school he founded in Minneapolis received national publicity almost immediately because one of the first dogs he trained served as guide and companion of Senator Thomas D. Schall of Minnesota. Soon the Master Eye Foundation became highly regarded. Using dogs of his own breeding, Mr. Sinykin established an outstanding school.

Having a guide dog is not practical for every sightless person. With approximately 600,000 known blind in this country and with the cost of turning out a guide dog approaching $6,000, only a small portion of those who could be helped by a dog get the opportunity. Most schools receive assistance from fund drives, service organizations, or invested capital so that money is seldom a problem. There are, then, many other reasons we see fewer guide dogs on the street than we should like to see. For example, some people dislike dogs; others just cannot develop rapport with animals and do not want dogs. Families are often afraid to permit a sightless loved one to seek this means of freedom. Some are even ignorant of the availability of guide dogs.

When we consider the freedom and independence afforded a guide dog owner, we wonder why more people aren't holding on to harnesses as they go about a productive life. Perhaps there are not enough quality dogs being bred to supply the demands of the schools now in operation. If not, breeders could be, and should be, thinking of ways to assist these schools. Not all schools have their own breeding programs and some do accept dogs of certain exacting qualifications.

Search and Rescue

In the past ten years a movement has developed in this country that presents the German Shepherd Dog in another phase of his versatility. Here his curious nature, stamina, verve, intelligence, self-reliance and keen sense of smell are employed to the fullest. Searching for humans, hopefully alive, has become a highly specialized field for a great number of owners who find using their dogs in this area most rewarding. The parent group, called ARDA (for American Rescue Dog Association), is comprised of six units in Virginia, Washington, Wisconsin, New Jersey, New Mexico and New York. One of the groups employing only German Shepherd Dogs is SARDA or Search and Rescue Dog Association, based in Seattle, Washington. Under the driving force of the late Bill Syrotuck, with some financial assistance of the German Shepherd Dog Club of America, this group has become outstanding in capability and devotion.

According to Doug McClelland, writing in Issue #13 of *Rescue Dog Magazine*, "SARDA was pressed into its most difficult search when Mount St. Helens erupted on May 18, 1980. A total of nine missions from May 25th to September 1st were logged by dog and handler teams. Missions not only were very dangerous but highly technical in nature. Two helicopters per dog team (a scout chopper and transport chopper with support personnel from both Lewis and Cowlitz county SAR units) spent a maximum of 30 minutes at each probable search site. As the choppers and support personnel waited ready for emergency escape, dog and handler searched nearby abandoned vehicles and campsites for indications of human scent. In this uncontaminated environment SAR dogs were the most effective tool in locating the victims of the May 18th eruption. Removal of the bodies in the mix of ash, mud and downfallen timber proved an awesome task.

"One recent search occurred when SARDA was called to Grand Teton National Park in Wyoming to search for an overdue hiker. Dog teams searched from the 12,000 foot level on rugged Buck Mountain to the 6,000 foot valley floor below, as Park Service climbing rangers searched the technical routes of Buck Mountain itself. On day two of the search by SARDA (six days after the hiker was reported missing) a dog/handler team located the hiker, dead on a rock talus slope. He had fallen 2,000 feet in elevation from near the top of Buck Mountain attempting to climb the technical route to the summit."

Training for Search and Rescue must begin at an early age when imprinting by games of hide-and-seek, for one thing, much socializing, walks and romps over rough terrain, accustom the puppy to what he will encounter later. Puppies must be sure to sound, learn to climb ladders (to get into airplanes), adjust to riding in helicopters, be amiable around other dogs in close quarters, and above all, be sound physically and mentally.

It requires at least one and one-half years (600–1,000 hours) of training, great amounts of money, to turn out a competent handler

Search and Rescue Dog Association dogs preparing for airlift. Note relaxed demeanor of dogs. Search resulted in locating 75-year-old-man, lost four days in woods of Virginia.

Rescue dogs from New York and Washington state units joined forces for a search in the Adirondacks in 1974.

and dog. Most work is volunteer by devoted people who feel their dogs can contribute to society by aiding at disasters, whether it be that of one lost child, earthquake, tornado or avalanche. At all times, the German Shepherd Dog air scents — he does not trail a track — off leash with his handler sighting him at all times. Scent travels 25 feet to one quarter mile, depending on wind and length of time, in case of death of victim.

Search and Rescue teams are called upon to assist sheriffs' offices, park rangers and military installations. Tales of finding lost children, wandering aged, and victims of disaster appear fequently in news reports. The work is phenomenal and should be supported by public funds so that more units could function nationwide.

One phase of Search and Rescue is the Avalanche Search program. This work began in the Alpine areas of Europe—in France, Switzerland, Austria and Italy—where there are 500 certified Avalanche dogs. In addition to basic Search and Rescue training, these dogs must learn to ride chair lifts and aerial trams.

A victim is found in an avalanche.

Dog and man work to dig out avalanche victim.

Soldier assigned to Army's Biological Sensor Research Group tests 16-month old German Shepherd Dog sire used in selective breeding program at Edgewood Arsenal (Maryland) to develop a better military dog.

Training German Shepherd Dogs at the EUCOM QM School for sentry duty.

Air scenting also is employed by these dogs searching under mounds of snow. A buried victim has a 50% chance of surviving for 30 minutes, but the odds are reduced to 30% and rapidly decrease to almost zero after one and one-half hours.

Military Dogs

In World War I, Germany's military employed about 1,500 German Shepherd Dogs, mainly in the Medical Corps and Message Service. In World War II, approximately 25,000 German Shepherd Dogs were drafted into service. Much of the breed's first popularity in this country arose from our "doughboys' " tales of German War Dogs of World War I. Intelligence, courage, extreme loyalty, keen senses, and great physical stamina make this breed irreplaceable in the military as many of our servicemen have discovered through World War II, Korea and Vietnam, and wherever troops have been deployed.

At the beginning of World War II, 32 breeds were listed as acceptable for service. However, by 1946 the German Shepherd Dog was adopted as the official breed for training. He adapts readily to military service for reasons stated above and for his ability to withstand variations in climate. A thick outer-coat over a dense under-coat provides excellent protection against heat, cold, water, insects, underbrush or thicket. Very little grooming is required to condition the coat and heavy hair permitted to grow between thickly padded toes provides additional protection. Although in some terrain leather boots have been used, German Shepherd Dogs usually do not require extra safeguards as they perform their varied military duties.

Individual categories in which dogs are trained are scouting, patrolling, tracking, mine and tunnel detecting. One particularly important aid for the infantry is the work of the Scout Dog that walks "point" similarly to the old Indian Scout we admired so much in Western movies. Here the dog's acute senses of smell and hearing far surpass that of his handler or a human "front Scout." Each dog alerts to his find in unique manner, so handler and dog must develop a close rapport. After a find is made, handler and dog retire to the rear — these dogs are not trained to attack the enemy, only to point to them. These tactical scout dogs have been responsible for saving thousands of lives in the Vietnam War alone.

Mine detector dogs work similarly but their expertise is ground scenting. Detection is made at least two feet from the mine location

A memorable photo—Ch. Arno of San Miguel, CDX, and companion.
—Courtesy, *German Shepherd Dog Review.*

An admiring gallery for dog being trained at ENT Air Force Base in Colorado Springs, Colorado.

and upon discovering the trap the dog sits at attention, alerting his handler.

Patrol dogs and tracking dogs work as they would in civilian situations. However, their work is far more dangerous in war time.

All dogs used by the military are recruited for the Department of Defense by the DOD Dog Center at Lackland Air Force Base, Texas. Here the dogs are processed and trained. In peace time, the majority are used for patrol in law enforcement and security work within the military. Additional training in narcotics and bomb detection is also provided.

Military dogs are never returned to civilian life but stay with changing handlers as necessary. Some dogs have worked at 12 and 13 years of age doing what they enjoy — using their natural instincts.

Pipeline dog "Avenger" checks a possible leak in Canadian oil field."

"Avenger" indicates a find by digging furiously.

New Services for New Times

In our complex society, many uses crop up for canine senses that surprise us, while others are mundane. We know of and possibly have seen the transit patrol dogs in subways and on subway trains. We hear of the occasional German Shepherd Dog that goes with a hunter and will retrieve the bounty on land or in water.

There are German Shepherd Dogs sniffing out oil leaks, gas leaks for Con-Ed, and now we have the Rock Hound, Jai, which has been trained to located sulphide-bearing rocks. Jai has a contract with St. Joe Minerals Corporation in New York to search out zinc, lead, and copper hidden underground. The idea for this program started with a Finnish Geological Survey. In 1970, training of several dogs was initiated and successful tests proved that a German Shepherd Dog is five times superior to man in discovering ore deposits underground.

In Movietone's storage vaults of old film, the breeds' keen sense of smell has been put to use in sniffing out bad acetate. "Duke" has been trained to locate rotting acetate so that infected film can be destroyed before the deterioration spreads. This German Shepherd Dog may help save thousands of feet of irreplaceable historical film.

We hear of dogs in Australia that are able to alert the countryside to oncoming tornadoes or "Willie Willies." Advance warnings enable stock men to move their cattle and sheep to safety. German Shepherd Dogs also signal the approach of the Australian desert-fires, often several days in advance. The breed is particularly restless at the onset of this storm and Australians heed the dogs' warnings.

The list grows and grows. As man, in his advancement, becomes involved in new and more intricate pursuits, the German Shepherd Dog keeps pace. He is indeed — as the *Deutsches Schaferhunde* standard prescribes he should be — the outstanding Working Dog.

Ch. Lord vom Zenntal, SchH, one of the influential German imports. Although used only for a short time in the United States for stud, Lord proved dominant for correct shoulder. He was later sold to Japan.

```
                                      Arko v Lenzfried HGH ZPr
                         Artus v Wilmstor PH
                                      Hilde vd Suhler Schweiz ZPr
              Bar v Oliverforst SchH II
                                      Odin v Busecker-Schloss PH
                         Ruma v Hans Schuetting SchH II MH
                                      Perla v Hooptal ZPr
CH. LORD v ZENNTAL SchH II
                                      Bodo vd Brahmenau ZPr
                         Gerbod vd Brahmenau SchH
                                      Ruth v Stolzenfels ZPr
              Dora vd Drei Galgen SchH II
                                      Etu vd Fuerstensalmburg SchH
                         Anita v Hengster SchH
                                      Alma Zum Goldenen Apfel SchH
```

9

The Breed in
Germany Today

P OSSIBLY the largest single breed organization in the world is the *Verein fur Deutsches Schaferhunde* (S.V.), located at Augsburg, West Germany. Here, all German Shepherd Dogs of that country are registered and full control over the breed is centered. Although the club is a member of the German Kennel Club, it is an autonomous organization, under the leadership of a president selected practically for life.

This highly organized, efficient operation is supported by 15 Regional Clubs, 1800 local clubs (*Landesgruppen*) and approximately 82,000 members. Financing is accomplished through membership dues and registration fees. In 1980, the club held 15 Regional Shows, 154 Specialty Shows and the Sieger-Hauptzuchschau or Champion Breed Show.

The S.V. exercises control over every aspect of the breed in Germany. Owners are advised how many times a sire may be used at stud, what bitches should be bred, whether an animal may be bred at all, what puppies should live, etc. Animals are approved suitable for breeding by official breed inspections. Strict rules are laid down — and followed — for breeding, training and exhibiting. Judges are educated and approved by the S.V., and their assignments, particularly inside Germany, are carefully scrutinized. When faults in the breed become too prevalent, judges are instructed to penalize dogs having them (as in the case of missing or additional teeth, occuring at present). If size becomes a problem, judges are advised to put up dogs so as to bring the size closer to the standard; breed wardens advise against using certain sires to overcome prevailing faults.

Contrast of American and German Controls

Periodically, a group in this country expresses a desire to adopt the system of breed registration used in Germany. Most recently, a group interested primarily in training for Schutzhund titles has expressed a desire to be dominated by an organization that has no authority here and has no influence with the German Shepherd Dog Club of America, or with the American Kennel Club, the principal registration organization in the United States.

In this country, the American Kennel Club recognizes *one* parent club in each breed. The parent club is a policy-making organization, with limited functions, operating under the rules of the American Kennel Club, which sets and protects the standard of the breed.

The German Shepherd Dog Club of America, Inc., parent club for our breed, conducts education programs, a Temperament Testing program, judging seminars, and attempts to direct the breed development through policies set down by the officers and Board elected by its membership. It holds Futurities, and puts on a yearly Specialty Show. It encourages training of dogs under American Kennel Club Obedience Trial rules and is interested in the development of Schutzhund training in this country. However, at present, the involvement is unofficial except for consenting for S.V. judges of trials and offering awards to members of the G.S.D.C.A., Inc. whose dogs attain titles.

Although Germany must be recognized as the "home land" of the German Shepherd Dog, breeders in this country feel little obligation to follow the policies of the S.V. and are not inclined to submit to any type of breed regimentation. However, it is suggested that we might follow the lead of German owners in conditioning and training our dogs so that we do not lose the special physical stamina and mental stability inherent in the breed.

GLOSSARY OF GERMAN TERMS

(Many of these terms, usually abbreviated, appear in German pedigrees.)

Abbreviation	German term	Translation
"a"		Indicating dog's hips have been certified normal.
	"Ablegen"	Lie down and be still!
	Abstammung	Origin, descent, ancestry
Abz.	Abzeichen	Markings
	"Achtung"	Look out! Watch! On guard!
	Ahnentafel	Pedigree
	Allgemeiner Eindruck	General impression
	Alter	Age
AK	Altersklasse	Open Class - with no training
	Angekort	Inspected and certified suitable for breeding
	Ankorung	Official inspection for breeding suitability
	"Apport"	Fetch!
	"Auf"	Up! (when the dog has been sitting or lying)
	Aufbeisser	Dog with even bite
	Augen	Eyes
A	Aureishend	Sufficient rating
	"Aus"	Out! Let go!
	Ausbildungskennzeichen	Standard
AD	Ausdauerpruefung	Passed endurance test
	Ausdruck	Expression
BDH	Bahndiensthund	Railroad service dog
	Behaarung	Coat, hair
Bes.	Besitzer, Besitzerin	Owner
	Bewertung	Qualification; value; rating (e.g. "excellent" "very good" "poor")
Bl.	Blau	Blue; slate-gray
	"Bleibsitzen"	Stay! Keep sitting!
B.F.H.	Blindenführer Hund	Guide Dog (for the blind)
Br.	Braun	Brown
Brgest.	Braungestichelt (Elchfarbig)	Elk color; mixed brown, not solid color
	"Bring"	Fetch!
	Bringen	To fetch
	Brustfleck	Spot on chest
	"Daun"	Down! Drop! (when dog off leash is to be halted at a distance from trainer)
	Deutsche Schaferhund	German Shepherd Dog
	Deutscher Reichsverband fur Polizei und Schutzhunde e. V.	German Reich Association for Police and Guard Dogs, Inc.

DSuchH	Dienstsuchhund	A tracker on active police duty
	Dressierung, Dressur	Training
D	Dunkel	Dark
Dr	Dunkelrot	Dark red
E.	Eigentumer	Owner
	Elchfarbig	Elk-colored; a brownish mixture, not solid tan or chocolate
	Ellenbogen	Elbows
	Eltern	Parents
	Enkel, Enkelin	Grandson, Granddaughter
	Erster	First
FH	Fahrtenhund	Tracking Dog
	Farbe, farbig	Color, colored
	"Fass"	Take it!
FCI	Federation Cynologique Internationale	International Dog Federation, which awards World Championship titles
	Fehler	Faults
F.	Fehlerhaft	Faulty
	"Fuss"	Heel!
	Gebrauchshund	Working Dog
	Gefleckt	Spotted
GB.	Gelb	Yellow
Gestr.	Gestrommt	Brindle
	Gewinkelt	Angulated
Gew.	Gewolkt	Clouded
	"Gib laut"	Speak!
	Glatthaarig	Smooth-coated
	"Gradaus"	Straight ahead! Forward! (for *gerade aus*)
	Grau	Gray
	Gross	Big, large
	Grösse	Size
	Grosseltern	Grandparents
	Grossmutter	Granddam
	Grossvater	Grandsire
G.	Gut	Good
	Haar	Coat, hair
	Hals	Neck, throat
	Hasenfarbig	Hare-colored, mixed brownish-gray
	Hauptgeschafstelle	Main office, headquarters
	Hell	Bright, light-colored
H.G.H.	Herdengrebrauchshund	Trained Herding Dog
	"Hier"	Here! Come here!
	Hinterhand	Hindquarters
Hr.	Hinterlaüfe	Hind legs
	Hirschrot	Reddish fawn
	"Hoch"	Up! Over! (command for jumping)
	Hoden	Testicles
	"Hopp"	Away! Over! (command for jumping)

	Höhe	Height
	Hund, Hunde	Dog, dogs (male, or in general)
	Hundin, Hundinnen	Bitch, bitches
	Inzucht	Inbreeding
JK	Jugendklasse	Youth Class
		(12-18 months for German Shepherd Dogs)
	Jung	Young
	Junger, Junge	Puppy, puppies, youngsters
JunghK	Junghundklasse	Junior Class
		(18-24 months for German Shepherd Dogs)
	Katzenfuss	Cat paw
	Kippohr	Flop ear
	Klein	Small
	Knochen	Bone
	Koer Klasse I	Especially recommended for breeding
	Koer Klasse II	Suitable for breeding. May be reclassified at a later date.
	"Komm"	Come!
	Kopf	Head
	Korzeichen	Breed Survey class
	Kräftig	Strong
	"Kriech"	Crawl! Creep!
	Kruppe	Croup
	Kurz	Short
	Langhaarig	Longhaired
	"Lass"	Let go! Out!
	Läufe	Running gear, legs
w H	Lawinen	Avalanche Dog
	"Legen"	Lie down!
	Leistung	Field training
	Lobende Erwahnung	Highly recommended
LG	*Landesgruppen Show*	Regional Club Show
M.	Mangelhaft	Passable, mediocre
M	Maske	Mask, face
MH	Melde Hun	Army messenger dog
M.	Mutter	Mother, dam
	Nachgewiesen	Indicated
	Naze	Muzzle, nose
	"Nimm"	Take it!
	Oberschlachtig	Overshot
	"Pass auf"	Watch out! Alert!
Pfsiz	Pfeffer und Salz	Pepper and Salt
	Pfote, Pfoten	Paw, foot
	"Pfui"	Shame! No!
	"Platz"	Down!
P.D.H.	Polizei Dienst Hund	Trained dog in actual police service
P.H.	Polizehund	Police-trained dog (of any breed)
	Preishunter Sieger	Sheepherding champion

	Rein	Pure, entire, solid (of color)
R.	Rot	Red
	Rucken	Back
R.	Rude	Male
	Rute	Tail, stern
	Salz und Pfeffer	Salt and pepper color
SH	Sanitätshund	Red Cross dog
S.	Sattel	Saddle
	Schecken	Parti-colored
	Scheu	Shy
	Schulter	Shoulder
	Schulterhohe	Shoulder height
	Schusscheu	Gun-shy
	Schussfest	Steady to gun
SchH I	Schutzhundprufung I	Working Dog Trial I
SchH II	Schutzhundprufung II	Working Dog Trial II
SchH III	Schutzhundprufung III	Working Dog Trial III
Schwz.	Schwarz	Black
	Schwarz mit braunen abzeichen	Black with brown markings; black and tan
	Schwarzgelb	Tawny; dark yellow
	Schwarzrot	Dark red
SG	Sehr gut	Very good (rating next below Excellent)
	"Setzen"	Sit!
S.	Sieger, Siegerin	Dog or bitch awarded VA-1 at annual Sieger show
	Siegerausstellung	Championship show
Sbgr	Silbergrau	Silver gray
	"Such"	Seek! Trail!
	"Such, verloren"	Seek a lost object!
SuchH	Suchhund der Polizei	Police Tracking Dog
	Tiefschwarz	Solid black
	Urgrosseletern	Great-grandparents
	Urgrossenkel, Urgrossenkelin	Great-great-grandson or great-great-granddaughter
	Urgrossmutter	Great-granddam
	Urgrossvater	Great-grandsire
	Ururgrosseltern	Great-great-grandparents
V.	Vater	Sire
	Vorderbrust	Forechest
	Vorderhand	Forequarters
	Vorderpfote	Forepaw
	"Vorwarts"	Go ahead!
V.	Vorzuglich	Excellent (highest rating)
W	Weiss	White
	Welp, Welpen	Young puppy, young puppies
	Wesen	Character, temperament, disposition
	Winkelung	Angulation

Ch. Arno v. Krenzwaldchen, one of the many great German imports brought to America by Ernest Loeb.

Vello zu den Sieben-Faulen SchH III FH

Jalk vom Fohlenbrunnen SchH III

Gunda vom Fohlenbrunnen SchH II

Frei vom Eichengarten SchH III

Dido vom Richterbach SchH II

Rita vom Wellstein SchH II

Anni vom Wokgaknie SchH I

CH. ARNO v KREUZWALDCHEN

Arras vom Adam-Riesezwinger SchH III FH

Klodo aus der Eremitenklause SchH III

Halla aus der Eremitenklause SchH III FH

Dorle vom Eichengarten SchH I

Dido vom Richterbach SchH II

Rita vom Wellstein SchH II

Anni vom Wolgaknie SchH I

	Zotthaarig	Shaggy-coated
SZ-Nr	Zuchtbuch Nummer	Stud Book number
ZPr	Zuchtpruefung	Recommended for breeding
Z	Zuchter	Breeder
	"Zur Spur"	Trail!
	"Zur Wache"	Watch! Guard!
	Zur Zucht nicht zugelassen	Not to be used for breeding
	Zwinger	Kennel

The 1969 and 1970 German Sieger, Heiko v. Oranien Nassau.

230

10

The Siegers
and Siegerins — Germany

EACH YEAR, in early September, thousands of devoted members of the S.V. from all around the world gather at the Sieger Show, to evaulate progress in the breed. This show is truly an "event", exciting and unique among dog shows. Rules are explicit and strictly enforced.

There are three classes in each sex:

Utility Dog Class — for dogs or bitches over 24 months old, with working qualification and a grade of Very Good or Excellent at a *Landesgruppen* show or a previous Sieger show.

Young Dog Class — for dogs or bitches from 18 to 24 months of age.

Youth Class — for dogs or bitches from 12 to 18 months of age.

Puppies under 12 months are not judged at regular shows, but are evaulated at regional surveys.

At the three-day event, all dogs are judged individually and those in the older group that are graded Excellent or Excellent Select on performance must have the "a" stamp for accredited hips, a SchH II degree, and pass a courage test in an adjacent ring. If this is not their first year in the Excellent Select class, dogs must have a SchH III degree. A full and perfect set of teeth is mandatory. Any dog over 3½ years old must have been surveyed and have acquired *Koer Klasse I* (especially recommended for breeding) status to be eligible for the Select rating.

Final judging of those that pass the courage tests occurs on the last day as thousands watch the top dogs of Germany and several foreign

A memorable picture of two of the all-time German Shepherd Dog greats in competition. At left, Ch. Pf fer v. Bern, handled by Ernest Loeb and right, Ch. Odin v. Busecker-Schloss, handled by Sidney F. Heck Jr. When Odin and Pfeffer were shown against each other at the German Sieger show in 1937, Pfeffer wc (Pfeffer had already been exported to America the year before, but was brought back to Germany for th Sieger show by owner John Gans. He is the only dog to have won Sieger and Grand Victor honors in t same year.) However, in two later confrontations in America, Odin was placed over Pfeffer each time a was to finish his career undefeated in the breed in this country. The two half brothers (both were sired Dachs v. Bern) complemented each other in physical attributes and the famous Long-Worth winn strain was founded on a combination of the blood of these two dogs together with that of the 1936 Sieg Ch. Arras a.d. Stadt-Velbert.

countries compete for what are the most coveted awards in the breed anywhere.

Many factors determine the choice of Sieger and Siegerin other than actual structure and gaiting — pedigrees are studied, often breed wardens are consulted, and records of siblings are considered. If they are older animals, their records as producers may be examined. Rules at German Sieger shows differ greatly from those of the American Kennel Club because the S.V. attempts, through every means including judging, to set the pattern of the breed.

Up to and inclusive of 1937, a Sieger and Siegerin were chosen from out of the class. However, the feeling grew that this put an undue emphasis on the bloodline of just one dog and one bitch. To give recognition to other bloodlines, beginning in 1938, a group of dogs considered outstanding for breeding were selected each year rather than just one, and were called the *Auslese* or select group.

In 1955, the Sieger title was reinstated. The dogs of the *Vorzuglich Auslese* (Excellent Select) group are rated, and the dog that is VA-1 becomes the Sieger. Similarly, the bitch that is VA-1 becomes the Siegerin. The Sieger is chosen by the President of the S.V. who always judges the *Gebrauchshund Klasse—Ruden* (the Utility class for males).

From 1974 through 1977 the Sieger and Siegerin titles were not awarded, an unpopular decision of the S.V. In 1978, the titles were restored.

1936 German Sieger, Arras a.d. Stadt-Valbert, ZPr, an important force behind many early American pedigrees. By Eng. Ch. Luchs of Caera ex 1935-1936 Siegerin Stella v. Haus-Schutting. Imported to America by Maurice Rose.

233

GERMAN SIEGERS

1899   Jorg v. d. Krone
1900   Hektor v. Schwaben
1901   Hektor v. Schwaben
1902   Peter v. Pritschen, KrH
1903   Roland v. Park
1904   Arlbert v. Grafrath
1905   Beowulf v. Nahegau
1906   Roland v. Starkenburg
1907   Roland v. Starkenburg
1908   Luchs v. Kalsmunt Wetzlar
1909   Hettel Uckermark, HGH
1910   Tell v.d. Kriminalpolizei
1911   Norbert v. Kohlwald, PH
1912   Norbert v. Kohlwald, PH
1913   Arno v. d. Eichenburg
1914-1918   *Not Awarded*
1919   Dolf v. Dusternbrook, PH
1920   Erich v. Grafenwerth, PH
1921   Harras v. d. Juch, PH
1922   Cito Bergerslust, SchH
1923   Cito Bergerslust, SchH
1924   Donar v. Overstolzen, SchH
1925   Klodo v. Boxberg, SchH
1926   Erich v. Glockenbrink, SchH
1927   Arko v. Sadowaberg, SchH
1928   Erich v. Glockenbrink, SchH
1929   Utz v. Haus Shutting, ZPr
1930   Herold a. d. Niederlausitz, SchH
1931   Herold a. d. Niederlausitz, SchH
1932   Hussan v. Haus Schutting, ZPr
1933   Odin v. Stolzenfels, ZPr
1934   Cuno v. Georgentor, ZPr
1935   Jalk v. Pagensgrub, ZPr
1936   Arras a. d. Stadt-Velbert, ZPr
1937   Pfeffer v. Bern, ZPr MH 1

1955   Alf v. Nordfelsen
1956   Hardt v. Stuveschacht

1959 and 1960 German Sieger, Volker v. Zollgrenzschutz-Haus, ROM.

1972 German Sieger, Marko vom Cellerland.

1957 Arno v. Haus Gersie
1958 Condor v. Hohenstamm
1959 Volker v. Zollgrenzschutz-Haus
1960 Volker v. Zollgrenzschutz-Haus
1961 Veus v. Starrenburg
1962 Mutz a. d. Kuckstrasse
1963 Ajax v. Haus Dexel
1964 Zibu v. Haus Schutting
1965 Hanko v. Hetschmuhle
1966 Basko v. d. Kahler Heide
1967 Bodo v. Lierberg
1968 Dido v. d. Werther Konigsalle
1969 Heiko v. Oranien Nassau
1970 Heiko v. Oranien Nassau
1971 Arras v. Haus Helma
1972 Marko v. Cellerland
1973 Dick v. Adeloga
1974-1977 *No Sieger and Siegerin title awarded—*
only Vorzüglich-Auslese (Excellent-Select)
The Sieger and Siegerin title was reinstated in 1978.
1978 Canto v. Arminias
1979 Eros v. d. Malvenburg
1980 Axel v. d. Hainsterbach
1981 Natan v. d. Pelztierfarm

GERMAN SIEGERINS

1899   Lisie v. Schwenningen
1900   Canna
1901   Elsa v. Schwaben
1902   Hella v. Memmingen
1903   Hella v. Memmingen
1904   Regina v. Schwaben
1905   Vefi v. Niedersachsen
1906   Gretel Uckermark
1907   Hulda v. Siegestor, PH
1908   Flora v. d. Warte, PH
1909   Ella v. Erlenbrunnen
1910   Flora v. d. Kriminalpolizei
1911   Hella v. d. Kriminalpolizei
1912   Hella v. d. Kriminalpolizei
1913   Frigga v. Scharenstatten
1914-1918   *Not Awarded*
1919   Anni v. Humboldtpark
1920   Anni v. Humboldtpark
1921   Nanthild v. Riedekenburg
1922   Asta v. d. Kaltenweide, SchH
1923   Asta v. d. Kaltenweide, SchH
1924   Asta v. d. Kaltenweide, SchH
1925   Seffe v. Blasienberg, SchH
1926   Arna a. d. Ehrenzelle, SchH
1927   Elly v. Furstensteg, ZPr
1928   Katja v. Blasienberg, ZPr
1929   Katja v. Blasienberg, ZPr
1930   Bella v. Klosterbrunn, ZPr
1931   Illa v. Helmholtz, ZPr
1932   Birke v. Blasienberg, ZPr
1933   Jamba v. Haus Schutting, ZPr
1934   Grete a. d. Raumanskaule, SchH
1935   Stella v. Haus Schutting, SchH
1936   Stella v. Haus Schutting, SchH
1937   Traute v. Bern, ZPr

1955   Muschka v. Tempelblick
1956   Lore v. Tempelblick

1956 German Siegerin, Lore von Tempelblick.

1958 Siegerin, Mascha v. Stuhri-Gau.

1967 Siegerin, Betty vom Glockenland, SchH III.

1957   Wilma v. Richterbach
1958   Mascha v. Stuhri-Gau
1959   Assja v. Geigerklause
1960   Inka Grubenstolz
1961   Assie v. Hexenkolk
1962   Rike v. Colonia Agrippina
1963   Maja v. Stolperland
1964   Blanka v. Kisskamp
1965   Landa v. d. Wienerau
1966   Cita v. Gruchental
1967   Betty v. Glockenland
1968   Rommy v. Driland
1969   Connie v. Klosterbogen, SchH II.
1970   Diane v. d. Firnskuppe
1971   Kathia v. d. Rheinliese
1972   Kathinka v. d. Netten Ecke
1973   Erka v. Fiemereck
1974-1977   *No Siegerin title awarded*
1978   Ute v. Trienzbachtal
1979   Ute v. Trienzbachtal
1980   Dixi v. Nato Platz
1981   Anusch v. Trienzbachtal

"The friends thou hast, and their adoption tried,
Grapple them to thy soul with hoops of steel."
—Shakespeare (*Hamlet,* Act I, Sc. 3)

11

Health and Care

HERE YOU ARE, back home after having acquired an eight-to-ten week old furry puppy. Hopefully, you have purchased it from a reputable *private* breeder, one who is interested in selling acceptable representatives of the breed. There are hundreds of devoted breeders, some with a number of brood bitches, and also many who have one good bitch.

It is important for a new owner to know where the puppy has come from — to be certain of its ancestry via American Kennel Club registration and a certified four or five generation pedigree. This pedigree certificate *should be given you when the puppy is purchased,* and, if the puppy has been individually registered by the breeder, an American Kennel Club transfer of ownership form *must be given.*

If only the litter has been registered (make sure it has been!) and the individual forms have not been returned from the American Kennel Club, ask the seller for the registration numbers and names of the sire and dam, as well as the date of the birth of the litter. In this way, should your puppy's registration papers not be forthcoming within a reasonable time (a month is sufficient), you will have the information you will need when you contact the American Kennel Club, 51 Madison Avenue, New York, N.Y. 10010. Be sure to register your puppy in your name as soon as possible even though you are not presently interested in showing or breeding it. You could have a superior animal and change your mind later.

Breeder and purchaser should sign an agreement that specifies what responsibility the breeder will accept in the future as the puppy matures. Many members of the German Shepherd Dog Club of America sign a Breeders Code and adhere to the requirements therein. It would be to your advantage to inquire about this, for then there can be no question as to how far the breeder will assume responsibility for the puppy.

The breeders' code to which German Shepherd Dog Club of America members subscribe reads as follows:

In keeping with my dedication to further the betterment of the German Shepherd Dog breed, I herewith pledge to maintain the following minimum practices:

1. To maintain the best possible standards of health and care in my kennels.

2. To refuse to sell or to recommend unethical breeders and unethical wholesalers or retailers, nor to sell to any buyer where I have reason to believe that the puppy or dog will not be properly cared for.

3. To keep and pass on to the buyers of puppies or adult dogs accurate health, breeding, registration and pedigree records. Papers may be withheld or breeder's rights retained by mutual agreement in writing.

4. To clearly state to the buyer of a puppy or adult dog whether sale is of a "showable" or "pet" or other type.

5. To urge all buyers to have a puppy or adult dog sold by me examined by a licensed veterinarian within 48 hours of receipt. Said examination to be paid for by myself or as previously agreed.

6. To deliver or ship only puppies or adult dogs of sound health and temperament. Where the buyer or his authorized representative did not personally see and choose the puppy or adult dog shipped by me, a period of 48 hours is granted to return or advise that he will return the animal promptly. Such return shipment to be at the buyer's expense or as previously agreed.

7. To use sales contract or written agreement to cover any sale or purchase involving a dog is mandatory. The sales contract of-

fered by the German Shepherd Dog Club of America, Inc., which covers guarantees and agreements, or one similar to it, must be used with signed copy to each party involved. A 4-generation pedigree must be given by the seller to the buyer at the time of sale. The buyer should be informed that a certified pedigree may be obtained from the American Kennel Club for a fee.

8. To refuse stud service to any bitch I consider in poor health, of unsound temperament, or of having hereditary, show disqualifying faults. Nor shall I use a dog or stud who I consider has these failings. At time of breedings, an exchange of pedigrees must be made.

9. To allow one repeat stud service where a bitch has failed to conceive after being bred to one of my studs, if the stud is still in good health and available, and at such a time and place as mutually agreed upon by the owner of the bitch and myself.

Responsible breeders will clearly state their opinion as to whether or not the puppy has show potential.

Feeding Your Puppy

Many breeders will furnish a feeding schedule so that there will be less trauma as the puppy leaves his first home and his siblings. Feeding dogs can be highly individualized, but we feel that the diet used by the Cobert Kennels, owned by Ted and Connie Beckhardt, is a good one and easy to follow. With their permission, we share it with you.

Diet for 7-week old puppy

Breakfast: ¼ pound of chopped beef - raw
2 tablespoons of baby rice cereal
1 tablespoon of wheat germ cereal
1 cooked egg
1 bone meal tablet crushed
MIX with milk formula (heat formula).

Formula: 1 can evaporated milk
1 can water
1 tablespoon of Karo syrup

Lunch: 1/8 pound of chopped beef - raw
1 tablespoon of cottage cheese
1 tablespoon of wheat germ cereal
1 pet tab crushed
MIX with milk formula

Dinner: ¼ pound of chopped beef - raw
2 tablespoons of quick oatmeal
or 1 shredded wheat biscuit
1 tablespoon of wheat germ cereal
¼ teaspoon of Sodium Ascorbate (Vitamin C)
C)
MIX with milk formula

Bedtime: 2 ounces of warmed milk formula

If puppy finishes all the food, continue with these amounts until 9 weeks and then increase the meat to a pound a day. If puppy does not finish all meals, decrease the amount served until pup eats it all up, and then gradually increase amounts. You can add vegetables, yogurt, and other cereals or rice.

Tips on Care

When you purchase your puppy he should have been wormed for round worms. It is a good idea to take him the next day for a veterinary checkup. In this way you can be certain he is in good health. The doctor will advise you what shots will be needed and give you a schedule for worming. Do not neglect this important responsibility—you have invested in 12 to 14 years of future pleasure and are duty-bound to care for a dependent creature that will reward your care with devotion and joy.

An outstanding feature of the German Shepherd Dog is his naturalness. No cropping of ears or tail, no clipping, trimming, powdering of coat are necessary. He will need nails trimmed regularly, teeth cleaned, ears wiped out and brushing daily, if possible, to bring out a beautiful lustrous coat. The German Shepherd Dog is almost free of body odor. Other than that, you see what he is. He is not prone to many annoying illnesses if fed properly and checked-on regularly for parasites. However, there are problems in all breeds of dogs and further on we will deal with these in a general way. We know of no health problems that are peculiar only to German Shepherd Dogs.

All dogs, particularly puppies, should have plenty of sunshine and fresh air. Insufficient exposure to sun can result in rickets, so whenever possible an outdoor run should be constructed—one 20 feet by 40 to 50 feet with sides of heavy wire at least six feet high. German Shepherd Dogs develop into very good jumpers and fence scalers so that an overhang of one foot or better still, a complete wire cover is advisable. There are many portable runs available but one constructed of heavy gauge wire on metal pipes is serviceable. Be sure either to sink the wire into the ground or bury cinder blocks around the run to prevent your dog from digging out. Place the dog's house so that it opens toward the south. Also provide some outside wooden flooring so the dog has a dry place to lie. A shade table about two feet off the ground is a nice feature, particularly in hot areas.

A word of warning: do not feed young dogs in a gravel run. Often they will remove food from the dog pan and lay it on the ground or gravel, then eat it later along with some gravel. Many young puppies have died from obstructions caused by owners who are unaware of this danger. It is best to feed your puppy indoors where you can watch and encourage him should he be a poor eater.

Owners of German Shepherd Dogs rejoice in the fastidious cleanliness of the breed. There is no other breed so readily house-broken if owners will devote several days of consistent training. Puppies should be taken outdoors—to the same spot for a while—immediately after eating and after sleeping. Always use the same words to signal going out; always give praise for deed accomplished; always say "no" if your puppy begins to do something you do not wish, punish him by a soft slap and "Shame" if he has made an error. However, it is best not to use severe punishment because a young puppy must develop functional control and making him nervous only confuses him. Constant watching and consistent commands and punishment will do the trick in record time. For a time puppies should be confined at night where an accident will do no harm. Some owners, apartment dwellers usually, will paper train puppies. Where access to outdoors is easy, this method is unnecessary.

All kinds of friends from all lands. Photo brought back from Russia by Pam Cole, whose parents owned the famous Dornwald Kennels.

Health

Along with the usual health problems that all dogs are prone to (i.e. worms, fleas, hepatitis, distemper, ticks, intenstinal upsets, sore ears), there are several very serious physical problems that *can* develop. As mentioned earlier, a good veterinarian is a must to help you raise your puppy and care for an active robust dog. When you are in doubt about his health, do not hesitate to call the doctor for he may be able to prevent more serious trouble.

Canine Parvovirus

Of major concern since 1978, the disease known as *Parvovirus* has been under study at Cornell University at the Baker Institute's Department of Virology. According to an American Kennel Club release in March, 1981, the origin of the disease is unknown but the virus is related to feline panleukopenia and mink enteritis. Baker Institute has isolated the virus and after lengthy study has developed a vaccine that is safe and effective with immunity duration as yet unknown, but educated guesses put it at 18 months.

Since freezing does not kill the virus it is imperative that all feces in lawns or any exercise area be cleaned up to prevent spreading.

It is hoped that the vaccine developed by Dr. Leland Carmichael will produce long term immunity, making booster shots unnecessary. However, there is still much to learn.

If your dog suffers vomiting and diarrhea, get him to the doctor. Do not take a chance for this disease has a high fatality rate. Diagnostic tests are available to most doctors. This disease, unknown prior to 1978, has attracted a great deal of attention because of its epidemic possibilities. Dr. Leland Carmichael and Dr. Roy Pollock have made remarkable progress with subduing this insidious killer.

Panosteitis

Panosteitis, commonly called long-bone disease, runs in families and although painful it is not permanent. Dogs suffer lameness at

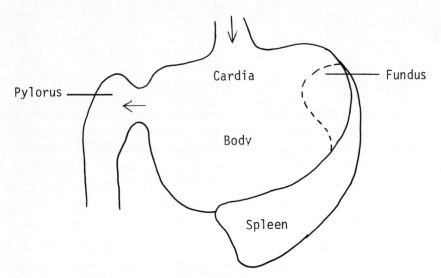

The normal position of the stomach and spleen.

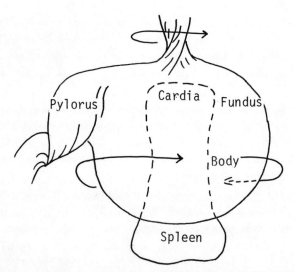

Bloat Syndrome: During volvulus, the gastric twist is greater than 180 degrees. This pinches off the inlet and outlet of the stomach and interferes with the blood supply to the stomach and spleen. Relief is imperative—*Drawings by Rose Floyd.* (Reprinted, with permission, from *Dog Owners' Home Veterinary Handbook,* copyright, Howell Book House, 1979.)

about five to twelve months, recover in several months with only treatment for pain prescribed. Occasionally a dog will lose some muscle strength. This disease, although not peculiar to the breed, has afflicted certain strains in it.

Pannus

German Shepherd Dogs may develop an eye problem known as *Pannus*. This disease is an invasion of the vascularized connective tissues in the superficial stroma of the cornea. It can affect both eyes and is characterized by a pink opaque membrane across the cornea. This condition usually occurs in older dogs and may lead to blindness. The cause is unknown but it is thought to be family-related. There is no permanent cure although the disease may be temporarily controlled if discovered at an early stage.

Canine Hip Dysplasia

Although the German Shepherd Dog breed has been singled out by the public and even some veterinarians, in the concern about *Canine Hip Dysplasia*, it is not the only breed where this disorder occurs. In fact, nearly all breeds are affected — especially so where adults weigh over forty pounds. Indication of the disease is lameness in the rear at about four to nine months. The only universally reliable diagnosis is done by X-raying the pelvis and hips.

The curse of this disease lies in its degree of hereditary penetration. If all dysplastic parents produced entirely dysplastic offspring, eradication might be possible. However, even dogs with normal hips can produce dysplastic litters or litters with several normal puppies among several dysplastic ones. If you request it, a veterinarian will send your dog's X-ray to the Orthopedic Foundation for Animals in Columbia, Missouri. The OFA charges a fee for experts to interpret X-rays and grade your dog's hips. If the X-ray shows normal hips the OFA issues an OFA number certified at twenty-four months or older. X-rays at an earlier age will be reviewed but no certified number is given to younger dogs.

Bloat or Gastric Dilation

In recent years, many outstanding show dogs as well as average pets have been lost to this dreaded disease. The condition has become more prevalent, particularly among males over two years of age. The stomach swells from gas or fluid and may twist 180° or more causing torsion. If it is possible, get your dog to the doctor at once. If not, and the dog cannot belch or vomit, insert a large bore needle into your dog's stomach immediately below the rib cage. The needle must go through the abdomen and into the stomach permitting gas to escape through the needle. It would be well for owners of large breeds to keep such a needle in the medicine cabinet. Although there are dangers for the layman in using such heroic measures, they could save your dog's life. The doctor still will be needed, as your treatment will be only temporary. Usually surgery is necessary.

Some studies show that eating large quantities of dry kibble, drinking large amounts of water, heavy exercising after eating can contribute to the onset of Bloat. To safeguard against it, close surveillance of your dog's eating habits could save him from severe distress, even be life-saving.

Spondylitis/Myleopathy

Many older dogs suffer from spinal inflammations — spondylitis — or myleopathy — degeneration of the spinal cord. This latter disease manifests itself in lack of coordination and often partial hindquarter paralysis. Muscles may atrophy but usually owners do not wish to see their older dogs unable to navigate and, since no cure is possible, have the dogs euthenized before the disease has progressed to complete deterioration. This disease, too, seems to be family related although not enough study has been done on the subject to prove this assumption.

We have reviewed briefly the unusual diseases that might afflict your dog. However, you may never need to know more than their names. Hopefully, with good care and barring any trauma, your German Shepherd Dog will live out his years bestowing his particular brand of devotion and loyalty in return for your concern for him.

GLOSSARY OF DOG TERMS

Achilles tendon: The large tendon attaching the muscle of the calf in the second thigh to the bone below the hock; the hamstring.

AKC: The American Kennel Club.

Albino: An animal having a congenital deficiency of pigment in the skin, hair, and eyes.

American Kennel Club: A federation of member show-giving and specialty clubs which maintains a stud book, and formulates and enforces rules under which dog shows and other canine activities in the United States are conducted. Its address is 51 Madison Ave., New York, N.Y. 10010.

Angulation: The angles of the bony structure at the joints, particularly of the shoulder with the upper arm (front angulation), or the angles at the stifle and the hock (rear angulation).

Ankylosis: Malformation of tail where several vertebrae are fused together causing a clumpy appearance of tail. A serious fault.

Anus: The posterior opening of the alimentary canal through which the feces are discharged.

Apple head: A rounded or domed skull.

Balance: A nice adjustment of the parts one to another; no part too big or too small for the whole organism; symmetry.

Barrel: The ribs and body.

Bitch: The female of the dog species.

Blaze: A white line or marking extending from the top of the skull (often from the occiput), between the eyes, and over the muzzle.

Brisket: The breast or lower part of the chest in front of and between the forelegs, sometimes including the part extending back some distance behind the forelegs.

Burr: The visible, irregular inside formation of the ear.

Butterfly nose: A nose spotted or speckled with flesh color.

Canine: (Noun) Any animal of the family *Canidae,* including dogs, wolves, jackals, and foxes.

(Adjective) Of or pertaining to such animals; having the nature and qualities of a dog.

Canine tooth: The long tooth next behind the incisors in each side of each jaw; the fang.

Character: A combination of points of appearance, behavior, and disposition contributing to the whole dog and distinctive of the individual dog or of its particular breed.

251

Cheeky: Having rounded muscular padding on sides of the skull.

Chiseled: (Said of the muzzle) modeled or delicately cut away in front of the eyes to conform to breed type.

Chops: The mouth, jaws, lips, and cushion.

Close-coupled: Short in the loins.

Cobby: Stout, stocky, short-bodied; compactly made; like a cob (horse).

Coupling: The part of the body joining the hindquarters to the parts of the body in front; the loin; the flank.

Cow-hocks: Hocks turned inward and converging like the presumed hocks of a cow.

Croup: The rear of the back above the hind limbs; the line from the pelvis to the set-on of the tail.

Cryptorchid: A male animal in which the testicles are not externally apparent, having failed to descend normally, not to be confused with a castrated dog.

Dentition: The number, kind, form, and arrangement of the teeth.

Dewclaws: Additional toes on the inside of the leg above the foot; the ones on the rear legs usually removed in puppyhood in most breeds.

Dewlap: The pendulous fold of skin under the neck.

Distemper teeth: The discolored and pitted teeth which result from some febrile disease.

Down in (or on) pastern: With forelegs more or less bent at the pastern joint.

Dry: Free from surplus skin or flesh about mouth, lips, or throat.

Dudley nose: A brown or flesh-colored nose, usually accompanied by eye-rims of the same shade and light eyes.

Ewe-neck: A thin sheep-like neck, having insufficient, faulty, or concave arch.

Expression: The combination of various features of the head and face, particularly the size, shape, placement and color of eyes, to produce a certain impression, the outlook.

Femur: The heavy bone of the true thigh.

Fiddle front: A crooked front with bandy legs, out at elbow, converging at pastern joints, and turned out pasterns and feet, with or without bent bones of forearms.

Flews: The chops; pendulous lateral parts of the upper lips.

Forearm: The part of the front leg between the elbow and pastern.

Front: The entire aspect of a dog, except the head, when seen from the front; the forehand.

Guard hairs: The longer, smoother, stiffer hairs which grow through the undercoat and normally conceal it.

Hackney action: The high lifting of the front feet, like that of a Hackney horse, a waste of effort.

Hare-foot: A long, narrow, and close-toed foot, like that of the hare or rabbit.

Haw: The third eyelid, or nictitating membrane, especially when inflamed.

Height: The vertical distance from withers at top of shoulder blades to floor.

Hock: The lower joint in the hind leg, corresponding to the human ankle; sometimes, incorrectly, the part of the hind leg, from the hock joint to the foot.

Humerus: The bone of the upper arm.

Incisors: The teeth adapted for cutting; specifically, the six small front teeth in each jaw between the canines or fangs.

Knuckling over: Projecting or bulging forward of the front legs at the pastern joint; incorrectly called knuckle knees.

Leather: Pendant ears.

Lippy: With lips longer or fuller than desirable in the breed under consideration.

Loaded: Padded with superfluous muscle (said of such shoulders).

Loins: That part on either side of the spinal column between the hipbone and the false ribs.

Molar tooth: A rear, cheek tooth adapted for grinding food.

Monorchid: A male animal having just one testicle in the scrotum; monorchids may be potent and fertile.

Muzzle: The part of the face in front of the eyes.

Nictitating membrane: A thin membrane at the inner angle of the eye or beneath the lower lid, capable of being drawn across the eyeball. This membrane is frequently surgically excised in some breeds to improve the expression.

Occiput or occipital protuberance: The bony knob at the top of the skull between the ears.

Occlusion: The bringing together of the opposing surfaces of the two jaws; the relation between those surfaces when in contact.

Just showing off

Olfactory: Of or pertaining to the sense of smell.

Out at elbow: With elbows turned outward from body due to faulty joint and front formation, usually accompanied by pigeon-toes; loosely-fronted.

Out at shoulder: With shoulder blades loosely attached to the body, leaving the shoulders jutting out in relief and increasing the breadth of the front.

Overshot: Having the lower jaw so short that the upper and lower incisors fail to meet; pig-jawed.

Pace: A gait in which the legs move in lateral pairs, the animal supported alternately by the right and left legs.

Pad: The cushion-like, tough sole of the foot.

Pastern: That part of the foreleg between the pastern joint and the foot; sometimes incorrectly used for pastern joint.

Period of gestation: The duration of pregnancy, about 63 days in the dog.

Puppy: Technically, a dog under a year in age.

Quarters: The two hind legs taken together.

Roach-back: An arched or convex spine, the curvature rising gently behind the withers and carrying over the loins; wheel-back.

Roman nose: The convex curved top line of the muzzle.

Scapula: The shoulder blade.

Scissors bite: A bite in which the incisors of the upper jaw just overlap and play upon those of the lower jaw.

Slab sides: Flat sides with insufficient spring of ribs.

Snipey: Snipe-nosed, said of a muzzle too sharply pointed, narrow, or weak.

Spay: To render a bitch sterile by the surgical removal of her ovaries; to castrate a bitch.

Specialty club: An organization to sponsor and forward the interests of a single breed.

Specialty show: A dog show confined to a single breed.

Spring: The roundness of ribs.

Stifle or stifle joint: The joint next above the hock, and near the flank, in the hind leg; the joint corresponding to the knee in man.

Stop: The depression or step between the forehead and the muzzle between the eyes.

Straight hocks: Hocks lacking bend or angulation.

Straight shoulders: Shoulder formation with blades too upright, with angle greater than 90° with bone of upper arm.

Substance: Strength of skeleton, and weight of solid musculature.

Sway-back: A spine with sagging, concave curvature from withers to pelvis.

Thorax: The part of the body between the neck and the abdomen, and supported by the ribs and sternum.

Throaty: Possessing a superfluous amount of skin under the throat.

Undercoat: A growth of short, fine hair, or pile, partly or entirely concealed by the coarser top coat which grows through it.

Undershot: Having the lower incisor teeth projecting beyond the upper ones when the mouth is closed; the opposite to overshot; prognathous; underhung.

Upper arm: The part of the dog between the elbow and point of shoulder.

Weaving: Crossing the front legs one over the other in action.

Withers: The part between the shoulder bones at the base of the neck; the point from which the height of a dog is usually measured.

WHATEVER would we do without tomorrow? The past, though usually nice to remember, is over and done with. The present is always tugging at us. But tomorrow — that is the dreamer's paradise. Everything is possible with tomorrow: no dream too foolish, no goal too high.

—Anonymous

BIBLIOGRAPHY

ALL OWNERS of pure-bred dogs will benefit themselves and their dogs by enriching their knowledge of breeds and of canine care, training, breeding, psychology and other important aspects of dog management. The following list of books covers further reading recommended by judges, veterinarians, breeders, trainers and other authorities. Books may be obtained at the finer book stores and pet shops, or through Howell Book House Inc., publishers, New York.

Breed Books

AFGHAN HOUND, Complete	Miller & Gilbert
AIREDALE, New Complete	Edwards
ALASKAN MALAMUTE, Complete	Riddle & Seeley
BASSET HOUND, Complete	Braun
BEAGLE, Complete	Noted Authorities
BLOODHOUND, Complete	Brey & Reed
BORZOI, Complete	Groshans
BOXER, Complete	Denlinger
BRITTANY SPANIEL, Complete	Riddle
BULLDOG, New Complete	Hanes
BULL TERRIER, New Complete	Eberhard
CAIRN TERRIER, Complete	Marvin
CHESAPEAKE BAY RETRIEVER, Complete	Cherry
CHIHUAHUA, Complete	Noted Authorities
COCKER SPANIEL, New	Kraeuchi
COLLIE, Complete	Official Publication of the Collie Club of America
DACHSHUND, The New	Meistrell
DALMATIAN, The	Treen
DOBERMAN PINSCHER, New	Walker
ENGLISH SETTER, New Complete	Tuck, Howell & Graef
ENGLISH SPRINGER SPANIEL, New	Goodall & Gasow
FOX TERRIER, New Complete	Silvernail
GERMAN SHEPHERD DOG, Complete	Bennett
GERMAN SHORTHAIRED POINTER, New	Maxwell
GOLDEN RETRIEVER, Complete	Fischer
GREAT DANE, New Complete	Noted Authorities
GREAT DANE, The—Dogdom's Apollo	Draper
GREAT PYRENEES, Complete	Strang & Giffin
IRISH SETTER, New	Thompson
IRISH WOLFHOUND, Complete	Starbuck
KEESHOND, Complete	Peterson
LABRADOR RETRIEVER, Complete	Warwick
LHASA APSO, Complete	Herbel
MINIATURE SCHNAUZER, Complete	Eskrigge
NEWFOUNDLAND, New Complete	Chern
NORWEGIAN ELKHOUND, New Complete	Wallo
OLD ENGLISH SHEEPDOG, Complete	Mandeville
PEKINGESE, Quigley Book of	Quigley
PEMBROKE WELSH CORGI, Complete	Sargent & Harper
POMERANIAN, New Complete	Ricketts
POODLE, New Complete	Hopkins & Irick
POODLE CLIPPING AND GROOMING BOOK, Complete	Kalstone
PULI, Complete	Owen
SAMOYED, Complete	Ward
SCHIPPERKE, Official Book of	Root, Martin, Kent
SCOTTISH TERRIER, New Complete	Marvin
SHETLAND SHEEPDOG, The New	Riddle
SHIH TZU, The (English)	Dadds
SIBERIAN HUSKY, Complete	Demidoff
TERRIERS, The Book of All	Marvin
WEST HIGHLAND WHITE TERRIER, Complete	Marvin
WHIPPET, Complete	Pegram
YORKSHIRE TERRIER, Complete	Gordon & Bennett

Breeding

ART OF BREEDING BETTER DOGS, New	Onstott
BREEDING YOUR SHOW DOG, Joy of	Seranne
HOW TO BREED DOGS	Whitney
HOW PUPPIES ARE BORN	Prine
INHERITANCE OF COAT COLOR IN DOGS	Little

Care and Training

DOG OBEDIENCE, Complete Book of	Saunders
NOVICE, OPEN AND UTILITY COURSES	Saunders
DOG CARE AND TRAINING FOR BOYS AND GIRLS	Saunders
DOG NUTRITION, Collins Guide to	Collins
DOG TRAINING FOR KIDS	Benjamin
DOG TRAINING, Koehler Method of	Koehler
GO FIND! Training Your Dog to Track	Davis
GUARD DOG TRAINING, Koehler Method of	Koehler
OPEN OBEDIENCE FOR RING, HOME AND FIELD, Koehler Method of	Koehler
SPANIELS FOR SPORT (English)	Radcliffe
STONE GUIDE TO DOG GROOMING FOR ALL BREEDS	Stone
SUCCESSFUL DOG TRAINING, The Pearsall Guide to	Pearsall
TOY DOGS, Kalstone Guide to Grooming All	Kalstone
TRAINING THE RETRIEVER	Kersley
TRAINING YOUR DOG TO WIN OBEDIENCE TITLES,	Morsell
TRAIN YOUR OWN GUN DOG, How to	Goodall
UTILITY DOG TRAINING, Koehler Method of	Koehler
VETERINARY HANDBOOK, Dog Owner's Home	Carlson & Giffin

General

COMPLETE DOG BOOK, The	Official Publication of American Kennel Club
DISNEY ANIMALS, World of	Koehler
DOG IN ACTION, The	Lyon
DOG BEHAVIOR, New Knowledge of	Pfaffenberger
DOG JUDGE'S HANDBOOK	Tietjen
DOG JUDGING, Nicholas Guide to	Nicholas
DOG PEOPLE ARE CRAZY	Riddle
DOG PSYCHOLOGY	Whitney
DOG STANDARDS ILLUSTRATED	
DOGSTEPS, Illustrated Gait at a Glance	Elliott
ENCYCLOPEDIA OF DOGS, International	Dangerfield, Howell & Riddle
JUNIOR SHOWMANSHIP HANDBOOK	Brown & Mason
MY TIMES WITH DOGS	Fletcher
OUR PUPPY'S BABY BOOK (blue or pink)	
RICHES TO BITCHES	Shattuck
SUCCESSFUL DOG SHOWING, Forsyth Guide to	Forsyth
TRIM, GROOM AND SHOW YOUR DOG, How to	Saunders
WHY DOES YOUR DOG DO THAT?	Bergman
WILD DOGS in Life and Legend	Riddle
WORLD OF SLED DOGS, From Siberia to Sport Racing	Coppinger